THE HANDY GUIDE TO ABBREVIATIONS AND ACRONYMS
FOR THE AUTOMATED OFFICE

THE HANDY GUIDE TO ABBREVIATIONS AND ACRONYMS FOR THE AUTOMATED OFFICE

Mark W. Greenia

SELF-COUNSEL SERIES

International Self-Counsel Press Ltd. Self-Counsel Press Inc.
Vancouver   Toronto   Seattle

Printed in Canada

Printed in Canada

First edition: April, 1986

Cataloguing in Publication Data

Greenia, Mark W.
    The handy guide to abbreviations and acronyms for the
automated office

  (Self-counsel series)
  ISBN 0-88908-629-X

  1. Abbreviations, English. 2. Acronyms.
I. Title. II. Series.
PE1693.G74 1986   423'.1   C86-091105-5

Cover design by Sara Woodwark

SELF-COUNSEL SERIES

International Self-Counsel Press Ltd.
Editorial Office
305 West 25th Street,
North Vancouver,
British Columbia V7N 2G1
Canada

Self-Counsel Press Inc.
1303 N. Northgate Way,
Seattle,
Washington, 98133 U.S.A.
(a subsidiary of International
Self-Counsel Press Ltd.)

To Kathy, Bridgette, and Pablo

CONTENTS

INTRODUCTION

This guide was compiled to provide a ready reference to the rapidly expanding number of abbreviations and acronyms in use in today's business and professional world. It contains over 7,500 entries, organized into 10 subject areas: information processing technical terms; information processing organizations; business and the law; medicine; industry and science; titles, degrees, and appellations; U.S. states and Canadian provinces; streets and addresses; chemical elements; and special symbols. Entries are organized in alphabetical sequence by acronym. The final section contains a list of specialized reference books and suggestions for further reading in the field of information processing.

(a) Definitions

An abbreviation is a shortened form of a word or words: for example, "addr" for "address" or "cont" for "continuous."

An acronym is a word formed from the initial letter or letters of a series of words: for example, "COBOL" for "Common Business Oriented Language," or "SYSGEN" for "System Generation."

(b) Alphabetization

The abbreviations and acronyms in this book are listed in alphabetical order. Where numerals form a part of the abbreviation or acronym, the entry is listed alphabetically as if the numeral were spelled out: for example, "4GL" is listed alphabetically as if it were spelled "Four GL."

In those cases where an abbreviation or acronym has more than one possible meaning, all meanings are listed alphabetically within the entry.

(c) Punctuation

Entries in the first two sections on information processing terms are for the most part capitalized, according to common usage. Terms such as "high frequency," which

can appear as "HF," "Hf," "hf," or "h/f," are here capitalized for uniformity. Terms that appear in common usage
in lower case only are listed in lower case: for example,
"mm" for "millimeter," "mm/dd/yy" for "month/
day/year."

Many abbreviations and acronyms appear both with
and without periods, hyphens, or slash marks (virgules).
For example, "cash on delivery" may appear as "COD,"
"C.O.D.," or "C/O/D," and "doing business as" may
appear as "dba," "d.b.a.," or "d/b/a." The practice in this
book is to omit these marks except where absolutely
necessary for use.

(d) Duplication

Every effort has been made to avoid duplication of terms.
If you do not find the abbreviation you want in the first
section you consult, check the related subject areas elsewhere in the book.

(e) Latin terms

Some entries, especially in the legal and medical sections,
are abbreviations of Latin terms. In those cases the term
is given with its Latin meaning, with the English translation given in parentheses. A letter "L" indicates a Latin
term.

(f) Registered marks

Some of the acronyms included in this book are the registered trademarks or service marks of a corporation or
business. In some cases they are indicated by "™," "®," or
"sm." However, the absence of such a symbol is not a
guarantee that the acronym is not a registered name or
trademark.

1

INFORMATION PROCESSING:
TECHNICAL TERMS

(Data Processing; Word Processing; Office Automation; Office Administration; Computer Systems; Business Computers; Telecommunications; Computer Personnel; Languages; Programs)

A

A accumulator; ampere; angstrom; area
AAIMS An Analytical Information Management System
AAS Advanced Automation System; Automated Accounting System
AAVD automatic alternate voice data
abbr abbreviation
ABC Atansoff-Berry-Computer; automatic bandwidth control
ABEND abnormal end
ABF application-by-forms
ABM automatic batch mixing
ABO advanced byte-oriented
abs absolute
ABT abort timer; answer back tone
ac alternating current; analog computer
ACA adjacent-channel attenuation
ACAP Automatic Circuit Analysis Program
acc accumulator
ACD automatic call distributor
ac/dc alternating current/direct current
ACE automatic computing engine
ACF advanced communications facility; advanced communications function
ACH Automatic Clearing House
ACI asynchronous communications interface
ACIA asynchronous communications interface adapter

ack acknowledgment
ACL access control list
ACR abandon call and retry
ACS Advanced Communication System; auxiliary core storage
act accumulator, temporary
ACTRAN Analog Computer Translator
ACTS Automatic Computer Telex Service
ACU automatic calling unit
ACV access control verification

AD average deviation
A/D analog/digital
ADA (A programming language, named after Augusta Ada Lovelace); automatic data acquisition
ADABAS Adaptable Database System
ADAM Advanced Data Management System
ADC air data computer; analog-to-digital converter
ADCCP advanced data communications control procedure
ADD authorized data distributor
ADDAR automatic digital data acquisition and recording
addr address
ADE automatic design engineering
ADF application development facility

ADIS Automatic Data Interchange System

ADL automatic data link

ADLC advanced data link controller

ADM adaptive delta modulation

admin administration

ADONIS Automatic Digital On-line Instrumentation System

ADP automatic data processing

ADPC automatic data processing center

ADPE automatic data processing equipment; auxiliary data processing equipment

ADPMC adaptive differential pulse-code modulation

ADPP Automatic Data Processing Program

ADPS Automatic Data Processing System; Automatic Display and Plotting System

adr address; address register

ADRAC automatic digital recording and control

ADRS A Departmental Reporting System

adrs address

ADRT automatic data recorder transcriber

ADS Accurately Defined System; address data strobe; Advanced Data Systems

ADS/O Application Development System/On-line

ADS-TP Administrative Data Systems -Teleprocessing System

ADT automatic data translator

ADU automatic dialing unit

ADX automatic data exchange

AE application engineer

AED algol extended design; automated engineering design

AEMS Airline Economic Modeling System

AESOP An Evolutionary System for On-line Processing

AF audio frequency

AFC automatic frequency control

AFG automatic function generator

AFL Abstract Family of Languages

AFO advanced file organization

AFT active file table

AGC automatic gain control

AHPL A Hardware Programming Language

AI artificial intelligence

AIDS Administrative Information Data System; Automatic Integrated Debugging System

AIG address-indicating groups

AIM advanced information management

AIRCON Automated Information and Reservations Computer Oriented Network

AIRS Automatic Information Retrieval System

AL Assembly Language

alap as late as possible

ALC airline link control; assembler language coding; automatic level control

ALD analog line driver

ALE address latch element

ALERT automated linguistic extraction and retrieval technique

ALGOL Algorithmic Language

ALP assembler language programming

ALPS Associated Logic Parallel System; Automated Library Processing Service

ALS advanced legal software

ALU arithmetic logic unit

AM administrative management; amplitude modulation

A/M auto/manual

AMC automatic message counting; automatic modulation control

AM-DBS amplitude modulation, double sideband

AMOS Advanced Mortgage On-line System

amp ampere

AMP asset management performance

AMPS Automatic Message Processing System

AMR automated management reports; automatic message registering

AMS Access Methods Services

AMSM Access Methods Service Macros

AMSSB audio modulation, single sideband

AMSU Access Methods Services Utilities

A/N alpha/numeric

ANACOM   analog computer
ANATRON   analog transistor
ANI   automatic number identification
ANT   active name table
AN/UYK   army/navy universal digital computer
AO   amplifier output
AO AMPL   and-or amplifier
AOC   automatic output control
AOS   add or subtract; Automated Office System
AOSP   Automatic Operating and Scheduling Program

AP   Applications Program
a/p   accounts payable
APA   all points addressable
APAR   authorized program analysis report
APC   advanced professional computer; automatic phase control
APD   angular position digitizer
APEC   automated procedures for engineering consultants
APG   automatic priority grouping
API   all purpose interface; applications program interface
APL   Algorithm Programming Language; A Programming Language
APOTA   automatic positioning telemetering antenna
APP   auxiliary power plant
APPC   advanced program-to-program communications
APS   Alphanumeric Photocomposer System
APSE   ADA Programming Support Environment
APT   all-purpose terminal; automatic picture transmission; automatically programmed tool
APTS   Automatic Picture Transmission System
APUHS   automatic program unit, high-speed
APULS   automatic program unit, low-speed

AQL   acceptance quality level

ARAM   analog random access memory
ARC   attached resource computer; automatic radio control; automatic relay calculator; automatic remote control
ARCS   Advanced Reconfigurable Computer System
ARD   advanced resources development
ARE   advanced real-time executive
ARIES   Automated Reliability Estimation Program
ARL   acceptance reliability level
ARM   automatic reel mounting; automatic route management
ARMA   autoregressive moving average
ARMS   Automated Records Management System
ARQ   automatic request for repetition; automatic retransmission queue
ARR   accounting rate of return
ARS   automatic route selection
ART   active reference table; automatic reporting telephone
ARU   audio response unit
AS   add-subtract; administrative support
asap   as soon as possible
ASC   advanced scientific computer; automatic selectivity control; automatic synchronized control
ASCC   automatic sequence-controlled calculator
ASCII   American Standard Code for Information Interchange
ASD   automatic synchronized discriminator
ASK   automatic shift keying
ASL   available space list
ASLT   advanced solid logic technology
ASM   allocation strategy module
ASN   average sample number
ASP   attached support processor; automatic servo plotter; automatic switching panel
ASPEN   Automated Speech Exchange Network
ASR   automatic send/receive
AST   active segment table
ASV   automatic self-verification
AT   automatic ticketing
A/T   action time
ATDM   asynchronous time-division multiplexing
ATE   automatic test equipment

ATL automated tape library

ATM automatic teller machine

ATMS Administrative Terminal Management System

ATR advanced technology printing

ATS Administrative Terminal System; Automated Telemetry System; Automatic Test System

ATT-IS AT&T Information Systems

AUTOPIC Automatic Personal Identification Code

AVD alternate voice/data

AVE automatic volume expansion

AVL tree Adel'son, Vel'skii and Landis (Binary Search) Tree

AX automatic transmission

B

b blank; block; binary; bit

BA binary add

BAC binary asymmetric channel

BACE BASIC Automatic Checkout Equipment

BADC binary asymmetric dependent channel

BAL BASIC Assembly Language

BALGOL Burroughs Algebraic Compiler

BAM BASIC Access Method

BAP band amplitude product; BASIC Assembly Program

BAR buffer address register

BASE Bank America Systems Engineering

BASIC Bank Automated Service Information System; Basic Automatic Stored Instruction Computer; Beginners All-purpose Symbolic Instruction Code (PC language)

BASIS Burroughs Applied Statistical Inquiry System

BBD bucket brigade device

BBL BASIC Business Language

BBM break before make

BBS (Electronic) Bulletin Board System

BC binary code; broadcast control

BCC block check character

BCD binary coded decimal

BCDIC Binary Coded Decimal Information Code

BCFSK binary coded frequency shift keying

BCH binary coded hollerith; Bose-Chandhuri-Hocquenghem Code

BCI binary coded information; broadcast interference

BCM basic control monitor

BCO binary coded octal

BCOM Burroughs Computer Output to Microfilm

BCP byte control protocol

BCPL Basis Combined Programming Language; Bootstrap Combined Programming Language

BCTR bright cathode ray tube

BCU binary counting unit

BCW buffer control ward

BD binary decoder; binary divide

BD binary to decimal

BDAM Basic Direct Access Method

BDC binary decimal counter

BDD binary to decimal decoder

BDH bearing, distance and heading

BDLC Burroughs Data Link Control

BDN Bell Data Network

BDOS BASIC Disk Operating System

BDP business data processing

BDU basic display unit

BE band elimination

BEAM Burroughs Electronic Accounting Machine

BEAMOS Beam Accessed MOS

BEE business efficiency exhibition

BEEF Business and Engineering Enriched FORTRAN

BER binary error rate; bit error rate

BERM binary entity-relationship model

BERT bit error rate test

BEST Business EDP Systems Technique; Business Electronic Systems

Technique; Business Equipment Software Techniques
BEX broadside exchange
BFD basic file directory
BFG beat-frequency oscillator
BFS BASIC File System
BH binary to hexidecimal

BI blanking input
BICS Burroughs Inventory Control System
BIDEC binary to decimal converter
BIM beginning-of-information marker; Business Inventory Management System
BINAC binary automatic computer; binary northrop automatic computer
BIOS basic input-output system
BIPCO built-in place components
BIPED Business Education for the Disabled
BIRS BASIC Indexing and Retrieval System
BISAM BASIC Indexed Sequential Access Method
BISYNC binary synchronous communications
BIT business information terminal; binary digit; built-in test
BITN Bilateral Iterative Network
BIT/SEC binary digits per second
BIVAR bivariant function generator
BIX Binary Information Exchange

BJF batch job foreground
BJM between job monitor
bksp backspace

bl blanking
BLADE BASIC Level Automation of Data Through Electronics
BLADES Bell Laboratories Automatic Design System
BLF bubble lattice file
BLIS Bell Laboratories Interpretive System
blk block
blksize block size
blnk blank
BLT BASIC Language Translator
BLU BASIC Link Unit; BASIC Logic Unit
BM buffer module
bmd biomedical

BMEWS Ballistic Missile Early Warning System
BN binary number
BNA Boeing Network Architecture
BNG Branch No Group
BNS Binary Number System
BO beat oscillator
B-O binary to octal
BOI branch output interrupt
BOLD Bibliographic On-line Display
BOM basic operating monitor
BOP Binary Output Program; bit-oriented protocol
BORAM Block Oriented Random Access Memory
BOS Background Operating System; BASIC Operating System
BOSS Business Oriented Software System
BOT beginning of tape
bp bandpass
BPAM BASIC Partitioned Access Method
bpf bandpass filter
BPI bits per inch; bytes per inch
BPM batch processing monitor
BPS BASIC Programming System; bits per second
BPSK binary phase-shift keying
BR break request
BRC branch conditional
BRD binary read
BRIL brilliance rate multiplier
BRS break request signal
BRU branch unconditional
BS binary subtract; branch standard
BSAM BASIC Sequential Access Method
BSC binary symmetric channel; binary synchronous communication
BSCN bit scan
BSDC binary symmetric dependent channel
BSIC binary symmetric independent channel
BSP Burroughs Scientific Processor; business systems planning
BST beam switching tube
bsy busy
BTAM BASIC Tele-processing Access Method; BASIC Terminal Access Method

BTD   binary to decimal
BTDL   BASIC-Transient Diode Logic
BTL   beginning tape label
B-tree   Balanced Multiway Search Tree
BTSP   Bootstrap
BTSS   BASIC Time Sharing System
BTST   busy tone start lead

BTU   BASIC Transmission unit; British thermal unit
buf   buffer
BUIC   back up interceptor control
bw   bandwidth
bwr   bandwidth ratio
BYP   bypass character

C

C   (A programming language, Bell Laboratories); centigrade; Celsius; character; compute; computer; control
CA   computers and automation; computer aided; computer assisted (*The terms CA, "computer aided," and CA, "computer assisted," are often used interchangeably. For the sake of uniformity in this text, the term "computer aided" will be used to cover both possible usages. For example, in CAE, "computer aided education," the additional translation of "computer assisted education" should be understood.*)
C&A   computers and automation
CAA   computer-aided accounting
CAAL   computer-aided adult learning
CACAM   Communications of the Association for Communicating Machinery
CAD   computer-aided design; computer-access device; Computer-Applications Digest
CADAR   computer-aided design, analysis and reliability
CADD   computer-aided design drafting
CADEP   computer-aided design of electronic products
CADET   Computer-Aided Design Experimental Translator
CADETS   Classroom-Aided Dynamic Educational Time-sharing System
CADIC   computer-aided design of integrated circuits
CADMAC   Computer-Aided Document Management and Control System
CADSS   Combined Analog-digital Systems Simulator
CAE   computer-aided education
CAFE   Computer-Aided Film Editor
CAI   computer-aided instruction

CAL   computer-aided learning; Conversational Algebraic Language
CALR   computer-aided legal research
CAM   central address memory; computer-aided makeup; computer-aided manufacture; content addressable memory
CAMA   centralized automatic message accounting
CAMAC   computer automated measurement and control
CAMP   computer-aided mask preparation
CAN   Computer Architecture News
CAP   computer-aided production; computer-aided purchasing
CAR   computer-aided search and retrieval
CARAM   content addressable random access memory
CARE   computer aided reliability estimation
CAT   compile and test; computer-aided teaching; computer-aided tomography; computer-aided transcription
CATS   Computer-Aided Training System
CATT   controlled avalance transit time
CATV   cable television
CAUSE   College and University System Exchange
CAW   channel address word
CBBS   Computerized Bulletin Board System
CBC   cipher block chaining
CBCT   customer-bank communication terminal
CBE   computer-based education
CBG   color business graphics

CBI compound batch identification; computer based instruction

CBIPO custom-built installation process offering

CBMS Computer Based Message Systems

CBT computer based terminal; computer based training

CBX Computerized Private Branch Exchange

CC card column; carriage control; central computer; closed circuit; condition code

C&C command and control

CCB channel control block

CCD charged coupled device; complementary coded decimal

CCDN Corporate Consolidated Data Network

CCF communications control field

CCIS common channel interoffice signaling

CCL common carrier line; Communications Control Language

CCLP common carrier line pool

CCP character controlled protocol; character count protocol

CCR central control room

CCS Continuous Commercial Service; Conversational Compiling System

cct circuit

CCT coupler cut through; custom computer technology

CCU central control unit; communications control unit

CCW counterclockwise

cd card

CD compact disk

CDC code directing character

CDCCP Control Data Communications Control Procedure

CDCE central data conversion equipment

CDD common data dictionary

CDE certificate in data education; certified data educator

CDF communications-data field

CDH command and data handling

CDI collector diffused isolation

CDK channel data check

CDL Computer Description Language; Computer Design Language

CDP certificate in data processing; checkout data processor; communication data processor

CDR call detail recording

CDT control data terminal

CDTS Centralized Digital Telecommunications System

CDU central display unit

CE channel end; computer engineer; customer engineer

CEI computer extended instruction

CEO comprehensive electronic office

CEP circular error probability; corporate electronic publishing

CEPA Civil Engineering Programming Applications

CF central file; certainty factor; conversion factor; count forward

CFB cipher feedback mode

CFR catastrographic failure rate

CG computer graphics

CGI color graphics indicator; computer generated imagery

CGP computer graphics processing

CHAIN Computerized Head-end Access Information Network

char character

CHDL Computer Hardware Description Language

CHIL current hogging injection logic

CHIPS Clearing House Inter-payments System

chk check

CHL current hogging logic

CHMOS complementary high performance metal oxide semiconductor

CI call indicator; circuit interrupter; control interval

CIA computer interface adapter

CICS Customer Information Control System

CIDF control information definition fields

CIF central index file; central integration facility

CIG computer image generation

CIM computer-integrated manufacturing; computer input from microfilm; critical index management

CIO central input/output multiplexor

cir circuit

CIS Computer Information Service

CIS-COBOL compact interactive standard for COBOL
CIT call in time
CIU computer interface unit
ck check
CKD count key device
CL Control Language; conversion loss
CLA communication line adapters
CLASIX Computer/Laser Access Systems for Information Exchange
CLASS Customer Local Area Signal Service
CLAT communication line adapters for teletypewriter
CLCS current logic, current switching
CLD called line
CLG calling line
CLIP Compiler Language for Information Processing
CLR computer language recorded
CLS Computer Letter Service; computerized litigation support
CLSR Computer Law Service Reporter
CLT computer language translated; computer line terminal
CLU central logic unit
CM computer module; communication multiplexer; control mark
cm communications
C/M communication multiplexer
CMC communicating mag card; communications control mode
cmct communicate
cmd command
CMF cross modulation factor
CMI Computer-Managed Instruction
CML current mode logic
CMMRR command mode rejection ratio
CMOS complementary metal oxide semiconductor
cmp computational
cmplx complex
cmptr computer
CMR common mode rejection, communications moon relay
CMS Communications Management Series; Conversational Monitoring System
CMV common mode voltage
C/N carrier to noise
CNC computerized numeric control
CNF conjunctive normal form

CNI Communications Navigation-Identification
CNL circuit net loss
CNM communication network management
COAX coaxial cable
COB complementary offset binary
COBIS Computer Based Instruction System
COBOL Common Business Oriented Language
COC coded optical character
CODEC coder-decoder
CODIC computer-directed communications
COED computer operated electronics display
COGO coordinate geometry
COGS cost of goods sold
COHO coherent oscillator
COIN complete operating information
COL Computer Oriented Language
COLINGO Compile On-line and Go
COLT communications line terminator; computer linked text; computerized on-line testing
COM computer output microfilm
COMAL Common Algorithmic Language
COML Commercial Language
comm communication
COMMCEN communication center
COMMZ communications zone
COMSAT Communications Satellite Corporation
COMSEC communications security
CO/NO current operator-next operator
CONS carrier operated noise suppression
cons console
CONSORT conversational system with on-line remote terminals
const constant
cont continue; continuous; control
COP coefficient of performance; Computer Optimization Package
COPE communications oriented processing equipment
COPICS Communications Oriented Production System
cor correct

corr correspondence

COS call originate status; Cray Operating System

COSMIC Computer Software Management and Information Center

COSMON component open/short monitor

cp card punch; central processor; clock phase; clock pulse; computer; control panel; control point; control program

CPC card programmed calculator; ceramic-wafer printed circuit; compact personal computer; computer power center; computer process control; computer program component

CPD cards per day; consolidated programming document

CPDD command post digital display

CPDS computer program design specification

CPE central processing element; central programmer and evaluator; customer premises equipment

CP/EM cp/m emulator

CPFF cost plus fixed fee

CPH characters per hour

CPI character per inch; computer-to-pbx interface

CPIF cost plus incentive fee

CPL Combined Programming Language; computer program library; Conversational Programming Language

cpld coupled

cplmt complement

CPM cards per minute; control program monitor; copies per minute; critical path method

CP/M™ control program for microprocessors

CPO code practice oscillator

CPODA contention priority-oriented demand assignment

CPOL Communications Procedure-Oriented Language

CPP card punching printer

CPR CAM plate readout

CPS central processing system; characters per second; Communications Processor System; Computer Power Systems; Conversational Programming System; cycles per second

CPSS Common Programming Support System

CPT Critical Path Technique

CPTA computer programming and testing activity

cpty capacity

CPU central processing unit

cpy copy

CQCF CICS Queue Command Facility

CQMS Circuit Quality Monitoring System

cqt correct

CR call request, card reader; carriage return; command register; control relay; control reverse; count reverse

cr credit

CRAM card random access memory

CRC carriage return contact; control and reporting center; cyclic redundancy check

CRF carrier frequency telephone repeater; control relay forward

CRJE conversational remote job entry

CRMR continuous-reading meter relay

CRO cathode-ray oscillograph

CrO₂ cromium dioxide magnetic tape

CROM control read only memory

CRP capacity requirements planning

CRTU combined receiving and transmitting unit

CRQ call request

CRS Command Retrieval System

CRT cathode ray tube

CRTU combined receiving and transmitting unit

CRYPTO cryptograph; cryptographic

CRYPTONET crypto-communication network

CS channel status; check sorter; chip select; computer science; control set; control signal; controlled signal; customer service; cycles shift

CSA common services area; computer system analyst

CSB complementary straight binary

CSD constant speed drive

CSDC circuit switched digital capability

CSDS Circuit-Switched Digital Services

CSE computer science and engineering; control systems engineering

CSECT control section

CSF critical success factor
CSI creative strategies international
CSL Computer Sensitive Language
CSM continuous sheet memory
C&SM communications and systems management
CSMA/CD carrier-sense multiple access collision detection
CSMP Continuous System Modeling Program
CSO chained sequential operation
CSP Commercial Subroutine Package; cross system product
CSSB compatible single sideband
CSSL Continuous System Simulation Language
CST channel status table
CSW channel status word
CT channel terminator; computer tomography; current transformer count; counter
CTA Channel and Traffic Control Agency
CTC counter timer circuit

CTAK cipher text auto key
ctpa coax to twisted pair adapter
ctrl control
CTS cellular telephone service; clear to send
CTSS Compatible Time-Sharing System
CT/ST cassette tape/Selectric typewriter
CU control unit
CUCB control unit control blocks
CUMREC College and University Machine Record Conference
CUSP Common User Program
CUTS cassette user tape system
CV constant voltage
CVSD continuously variable slope delta modulation
CVT constant voltage transformer
CW control word
CWP communicating word processors
CYBERNET (Network of Control Data Corporation)
CX character transmission

D

D decimal; density; digit; digital; display; doubleword; drum
DA data acquisition; data administration; data administrator; data available; decimal add; direct answer; discrete address
DAA data access arrangement; data authentication algorithm
DAC data acquisition and control; digital/analog converter
DACC direct access communication channel
DACS Data Acquisition and Control System
DACU device attachment control unit
DAGC delayed automatic gain control
DAL data access line
DAM Direct Access Method
DAME Data Acquisition and Monitoring Equipment for Computers

DAMPS Data Acquisition Multiprogramming System
DAP data access protocol; distributed array processor
DAPS Direct Access Programming System
DAR data access register
DART Daily Automatic Rescheduling Technique; data analysis recording tape
DAS Data Acquisition System; Digital Attenuator System
DASD direct access storage device
DAT dynamic address translation
DATACOM data communications
DATEL II (RCAs global communication data service in conjunction with TELENET)
DAV data available; data valid
DAVAR dealer authorized value-added retailer
db decible

DBA database administrator

d/b/a doing business as

DBC database computer

DB/DC database/data communications

DBM database management

DBMS Database Management System

DBRC database recovery control

DBS database service; direct broadcast satellite

DBTG database task group

DB2 database two

DC data channel; data communications; define constant; direct current; directional coupler; disc controller; display console

DCA document content architecture

DCAA dual-call auto-answer

DCB data control block; define control block

DCBD define control block dummy

DCC data communications channel

DCCU data communications control unit

DCD data carrier detect

DCE discounted cash flow; distributed communications facility; document composition facility

DCI data communications interrogate

DCM data communications multiplexer; directory control module

dcmt decrement; document

DCO digital central office; digitally controlled oscillator

DCP data communication processor

DCPS digitally controlled power source

DCPSK differentially coherent phase-shift keying

DCR data conversion receiver; design change recommendation; digital conversion receiver

dcr decrease

DCS Digital Computer System; Direct Coupled System; Distributed Communication System; Distributed Computing System

DCTL direct coupled transistor logic

DCU decade counting unit; decimal counting unit; digital counting unit

DCUTL direct coupled unipolar transistor logic

DCW data communication write; data control words; define constant with wordmark

DCWV direct current working volts

DD data definition; data directory; decimal divide; digital display; double density; drum demand

DDA digital differential analyzer

DDAS Digital Data Acquisition System

DDC data distribution center; digital data converter; digital display converter; direct digital computer

DDCE digital data conversion equipment

DDCMP digital data communications message protocol

DDD direct distance dialing

DD/D data dictionary directory

DDG digital display generator

DDL Data Definition Language; Data Description Language

dd/mm/yy day, month, year

DDP digital data processor; distributed data processing

DDPS Digital Data Processing System

DDRP dial dictation relay panel

DDS Dataphone Digital Service; digital display scope; Direct Dial Service

DDT digital data transmitter; Dynamic Debugging Technique

DE decision element; device end; dictation equipment; digital element; display element

dec decimal; decision

decit decimal digit

DECNET Digital Equipment Corporation Network

decr decrement

DED data element dictionary; double error detection

DED/D data element dictionary/directory

DEFT dynamic error-free transmission

del delay; delete

dem demodulator

DE-ME-DRIVE decoding memory drive

demod demodulator

dens density

DEPSK differential-encoded phase shift keying

DES data encription standard; differential equation solver; Digital Expansion System

DETAB decision tables

DEU data exchange unit

DF describing function; dissipation factor

D-F direct flow

DFA digital flaw analysis

DFC disk file check

DFCU disk file control unit

DFG diode function generator; discrete frequency generator

DFR disk file read; double frequency recording

DFSU disk file storage unit

DFT discrete fourier transform

DFW disk file write

DG differential generator; diode gate; double grove

dgnl diagonal

DGS Data Gathering System

dgt digit

DHE data handling equipment

DI data input; digital input

DIA document interchange architecture

DIAL Display Interactive Assembly Language; Drum Interrogation, Alteration and Loading System (Honeywell)

DIALOG (The business news, technical database service of Information Services Inc., A subsidiary of Lockheed Corporation)

DIAS Dynamic Inventory Analysis System

DIBOL Digital Business Oriented Language

DIBS Digital Integrated Business System

DIC data input check

dict dictionary

DID datamation industry directory; digital information display; direct inward dialing

DIF document interchange format

DIGEX disabled interest group electronic exchange

DIGICOM Digital Communication System

DIGRM digit/record mark

DIGRMGM digit/record mark group/mark

DIIC dielectrically isolated integrated circuit

DIM device interface module

DIOB digital input/output buffer

DIP display information processor; dual-in-line package; dual-in-line pin

DISA direct inward system access

DISAC digital simulator and computer

DISCON Defense Integrated Secure Communications Network

DISOSS Distributed Office Support System

div divider

DIVA digital input voice answer-back

DJIRS Dow Jones Information Retrieval System

DL data link; delay line; diode logic

DLC data link control; duplex line control

DLCC data link control chip

DLCF data link control field

DLE data-line escape

DLO data link occupied

DL/1 data language one

DLT data loop transceiver

dly delay

dlyd delayed

DM data management; data manager; delta modulation

DMA direct memory access

DMC digital microcircuit

DME direct machine environment; distance measuring equipment

DMED digital message entry device

DMEP Data-Network Modified Emulator Program

D-MESFET depletion metal semiconductor field effect transistor

DMF digital matched filters

DMI digital multiplexed interface

DML Data Manipulation Language

DMM digital multi-meter

DMOS discrete metal oxide semiconductor

DMS Data Management System; discrete memoryless source

DMSS Data Multiplex Subsystem

dmux demultiplex

DN decimal number

DNA digital network architecture

DNC direct numerical control

DNCS Distributed Network Control System

DO defense order; digital output

DOC data optimizing computer; direct operating cost

doc document

DOCS Disk Oriented Computer System

DOCUS Display Oriented Computer Usage System

DO/IT digital output/input translator

DOL Display Oriented Language

DOMSAT Domestic Satellite Service

DONOACS Department of Navy Office Automation and Communications System

DOPIC document of programs in core

DOPS Digital Optical Projection System

DORIS Direct Order Recording and Invoicing System

DOS Digital Operating System; Disk Operating System

DOV data over voice

DOW JONES™ Network of Dow Jones and Company

DP data processing; dial port; dial pulsing; digit present; disk pack; dynamic programming

DPC data processing center; direct program control

DPCM data pulse code modulation

DPD data processing division; data processing department

DPDT double-pole double-throw

DPE data processing equipment

DPEX Distributed Processing Executive Operating System

DPF data processing facility

DPG data processing group; digital pattern generator

DPI data processing installation; dots per inch

DPM data processing machine; digital pattern meter; documents per minute

DPMS Data Project Management System

DPR digital present

DPS Data Processing Service; Data Processing System; Data Processing Subsystem; Document Processing System

DPSK differential phase-shift keying

DPSS Data Processing Subsystem

DPST double-pole single-throw

DPU data processing unit

DQC data quality control

DQM data quality monitors

DR data recorder; data reduction; digital resolver

dr drive; drum

D/R direct or reverse

DRAM dynamic random access memory

DRC data reduction compiler

DRI data reduction interpreter

DRM digital radio meters

DRO digital readout; destructive readout

DROS Disk Resident Operating System

DRS data rate selector

DRT data recovery tester; diode recovery tester

DRV data recovery vehicle

DS data scanning; data set; data synchronization; decimal subtract; define storage; define symbol; device selector; disk storage; drum storage

D&S display and storage

DSA define symbol address; distributed systems architecture

DSAS Data Set Analysis System

DSB double sideband

DSC direct satellite communications; document service center

DSCB data set control block

DSCS Desk Side Computer System

DS/DD double-sided/double-density

DSE data storage equipment; data systems engineering; distributed system environment

dsgn designation

DSI digital speech interpolation

DSL data set label; Data Set Language; Digital Simulation Language

DSL/ALPHA Data Simulation Language/Alpha

DSLC data subscriber line carrier

DSM device strategy module; discrete source with memory

DSN data set name; Data System News; Distributed Systems Network

DSO data security officer

DSORG data set organization

DSR data set ready; digital stepping recorder; digital storage relay

DSS Decisional Support System; direct station selection

DS/SD double-sided/single-density

DSU data service unit; device switching unit; digital synchronization unit; disk storage unit

DSU/CSU data servicing unit/channel servicing unit

DSW data status word; device status word

DT data translator; data transmission; digital technique; down time

D/T disk/tape

DTDM digital terminal data module

DTE data terminal equipment

DTF define the file

DTG data time group

DTIB decision table information bulletin

DTL diode-transistor logic

DTM delay time multiplier

DTO dollar trade-off

DTP directory tape processor; distributed transaction processing

DTR data terminal reader; data terminal ready; daily transaction reporting; digital telemetering register

DTS Data Transmission System; digital tandem switch

DTTU data transmission terminal unit

DTU digital tape unit

DTUTF digital tape unit tape facility

DUAL Dynamic Universal Assembly Language

DUNS Data Universal Numbering System

DUT device under test

DUV data under voice

DVST direct viewing storage tube

DVX digital voice exchange

DW data word

DX document transmission

dx distance; duplex

DXC data exchange control

DYNANA dynamic analyzer

DYNSAR dynamic systems analyzer

DYSAC digitally simulated analog computer

DYSTAL Dynamic Storage Allocation Language

E

e electrical; electronic; element; enable; error

EA effective address

EAG equipment advisory group

EAM electrical accounting machine

EAN European article numbering code

EARN European Academic Research Network

EAROM electrically alterable read only memory

EAS Electronic Accounting System; Extended Area Service

EAX Electronic Automatic Exchange

EBCDIC extended binary coded decimal interchange code

EBI equivalent background input

EBPA electron beam parametric amplifier

EBR electronic beam recording

EC electronic calculators; engineering change; error correcting

ECAP Electronic Circuit Analysis Program

ECB electronic claims billing; event control block

ECC electronic computer concepts; emitter-coupled circuits; error correcting code; error correction capability

ECCM electronic counter-counter-measures

ECCR electronic cash and credit register

ECD electro-chromic display

ECDC electrochemical diffused collector transistor

ECL emitter coupled logic; equipment component list

ECLIPSE Electronic Clipping Service

ECLO emitter-coupled logic operator

ECM electronic counter-measures

ECME electronic countermeasures equipment

ECN electronic change notice

E-COM Electronic Computer Originated Mail

ECOS Extended Communications Operating System

ECP executive control program

ECS Executive Control System; extended core storage

ECTL emitter coupled transistor logic

ECX Electronically Controlled Telephone Exchange

ED electrical differential; error detecting; external device

EDA electronic differential analyzer; electronic digital analyzer; exploratory data analysis

EDAC error detection and correction

EDACS Environmental Data Access and Control System

EDC electronic desk calculator; electronic digital computer; error detection and correction

EDCOM editor and compiler

EDCS Engineering Document Control System

EDCW external device control word

EDDS Executive Data Display System

EDE external document exchange

EDF execution diagnostic facility

EDGAR Electronic Data Gathering, Analysis and Retrieval

EDGE electronic data gathering equipment

EDI electronic dissemination of information; electronic document interchange

EDHE experimental data handling equipment

EDOS Extended Disk Operating System

EDP electronic data processing

EDPC electronic data processing center

EDPE electronic data processing equipment

EDPEO electronic data processing equipment office

EDPM electronic data processing machine

EDPS Electronic Data Processing System

EDS exchangeable disk storage

EDSAC electronic delay storage automatic calculator

EDU electronic display unit

EDVAC electronic discrete variable automatic computer

EE electrical engineer; external environment

EEI essential elements of information

EEPROM electrically erasable programmable read only memory

EEROM electrically erasable read only memory

EFL emitter-follower logic

EFPH equivalent full power hours

EFTS Electronic Funds Transfer System

EGP electronic graphics processing

EHF extra high frequency

EHV extra high voltage

EIES Electronic Information Exchange System

EIP Executive Interface Program

EIRP effective isotropic-radiated power

EIS Electronic Information Services; end interruption sequence; Executive Information System; executive interface structure

ELD edge lighted display; electroluminescent display

ELIAS Expandable Level Interactive Application System

ELINT electronic intelligence

EL I extensible language one

EM electronic mail; end of medium

E/M electro/mechanical

EMAS Edinburgh Multiaccess System

EME emergency power engineering

E-MESFET enhancement metal semiconductor field effect transistor

EMI electromagnetic interference; electro-mechanical interference

EMIS Educational Management Information System

EML equipment modification list

EMP electromechanical power

EMR executive management responsibility

EMS Electronic Management System; Electronic Medical System; Electronic Message System

EMT electrical metallic tubing

EMWP extended–machine–wait state–problem state

END end of data

ENIAC electronic numeral integrator and calculator

ENQ enquiry character

ent entry

EO executive order

EOA end of address

EOB end of block

EOC end of conversation

EOD end of data

EODAD end of data address

EOE errors and omissions excepted

EOF end of file

EOJ end of job

EOL end of life; end of line

EOM end of message

EON end of number

EOP end of output; end of program

EOQ economic order quantity

EOR end of record; end of reel; end of run

EOS Electro-Optical System

EOT end of tape; end of transmission

EOV end of volume

EP end of program; entry point

EPBX electronic private branch exchange

EPC easy processing channel; electronic program control; embedded print command

EPIC Educational Products Information Exchange

EPROM electrically programmable read only memory

EPSS Experimental Packet Switching System

EPU electrical power unit

eq equalizer

eqp equipment

eqpmt equipment

equ equate

ERA electronic reading automation

ERM entity-relationships model

EROM erasable read only memory

err error

ERX electronic remote switching

ES electromagnetic storage

ESC escape character

ESD electrostatic storage deflection

ESDI enhanced small device interface

ESDN extended software defined network

ESDS entry sequence data set

ESE/UM expert system environment/virtual machine

ESI externally specified indexing

ESP early support program; electrosensitive programming

ESQL/C Embedded Structured Query Language and Tools for "C" Language

ESR   effective signal radiated
ESS   Electronic Switching System
ESSU   electronic selective switching unit
est   estimate
esu   electrostatic unit
ESW   error status word
ET   earth terminal; elapsed time
ETA   estimated time of arrival
ETB   end of transmission block
ETC   electronic transaction cycle; esti-
mated time of completion
ETD   estimated time of departure
ETHERNET   Communication Network
of XEROX Corporation
ETIM   elapsed time
ETL   ending tape label
ETN   Electronic Tandem Network
ETS   Electronic Telegraph System
ETX   end of text character
EURONET-DIANE   European Network-

Direct Information Access Network for
Europe
eval   evaluation
EVFU   electronic vertical format unit
EVPI   expected value of perfect infor-
mation
ex   execute
exam   examine
exch   exchange
EXCHANGE   An In-depth Financial
Database
exclu   exclusive
EXCP   Execute Channel Program
excp   except
EXD   external device
exec   execute; executive
EXNOR   exclusive-nor gate
EXOR   exclusive-or gate
EXTND   extended data transfer
extsn   extension

F

f   feedback; filter; fixed; frequency
FA   forced answer; fully automatic
FAC   financial administrative control
FACE   field alterable control element
FACS   Flexible Accounting Control Sys-
tem
FACT   Fully Automatic Cataloging
Technique; Fully Automatic Compiler-
Translator; Fully Automatic Compiling
Technique
FAM   fast access memory
FAMOS   floating gate avalanche-
injection metal-oxide semiconductor
FAP   Financial Analysis Program; FOR-
TRAN Assembly Program
FAR   failure analysis report
fax   facsimile
FBA   fixed block architecture
FBC   fully buffered channel

FC   file control; file conversion
FCA   functional configuration audit
FC&A   frequency control and analysis
FCB   file control block
FCDR   failure cause data report
FCFS   first come, first served
FCL   feedback control loop
FCP   file control processor
FCS   frame check sequence
FD   file description; floppy disk; full
duplex
FDC   floppy disk controller
FDM   frequency division multi-plexer
FDOS   Floppy Disk Operating System
FDP   Field Developed Program
FDS   Full Development System
FDX   full duplex transmission
FE   field engineers; format effector;
framing error
FEC   forward error correction

FEDSIM Federal Computer Performance Evaluation and Simulation Center
FED-STD federal standard
FEP Financial Evaluation Program
FET field effect transistor
Fe²O³ ferric oxide

FF fixed fee; form feed
F-F flip-flop
FFT fast fourier transform
FGND frame ground
FHD fixed-head disk
FIFO first in, first out; floating input-floating output
fig figure
FIGS figure shift
FILO first-in, last-out
FIPS federal information processing standards
FK function key

FLBIN floating-point binary
fld field
FLDEC floating-point decimal
FLIH first level interrupt handler
FL/1 function language one
FM file maintenance; frequency modulation
fm format
FME frequency measuring equipment
FMEVA floating point means and variance
FMFB frequency modulation with feedback
FMS File Management System; Forms Management System; FORTRAN Monitor System
fmt format

FOC fiber optics communications
FOIL File Oriented Interpretive Language

F1 function key number one *("F" followed by a number usually indicates a function key on a computer terminal keyboard. There are often several of these, numbered "F1" to "F9," for example. The same is true for "PF" which stands for "program function key" and is often seen as "PF1," "PF2," "PF3," etc.)*

FOPT fiber optic photo transfer
FORMAC formula manipulation compiler
FORTRAN Formula Translation
FOSDIC Film Optical Sensing Device for Input to Computers
FOSE Federal Office Systems Exposition
FOUR GL fourth generation language
FP file protect; fixed point
FPAP floating point array processor
FPE Fortran programming environment
FPGA field programmable gate array
FPLA field programmable logic array
FPLS field programmable logic sequencer
FPM feet per minute
FPP floating point package
FPS feet per second; floating point systems; frames per second
FS file separator
FSA finite state automation
FSC full scale range
FSCM federal supply code for manufacture
FSB free storage block
FSBPRT free storage block pointer
FSBSEM free storage block semiphore
FSK frequency shift keying
FSM finite state machine
FSR feedback shift register
FT fault tolerant; full time; functional test
FTC frequency time control
FTM Fault Tolerant Multiprocessor System
FTP file transfer program
FTS federal telecommunications system; file transfer support
FTSC fault tolerant spaceborne computer
fun function
F/V frequency to voltage converter
FX foreign exchange
FXBIN fixed binary translation
FY fiscal year

G

g giga- (prefix, meaning "one billion"); ground

GaAs gallium arsenide

GAM Graphic Access Method

GAMA Graphics Assisted Management Application

GAN Generating and Analyzing Networks

GAP General Assembly Program

GAR Growth Analysis and Review

GASP Gas Plasma Display; General Activity Simulation Program; Generalized Academic Simulation Program

GATE Generalized Access to X.25 Transport Extension

gb gigabyte

GC guidance computer

GCD greatest common divisor

GCOS general comprehensive operating supervisor

GCR group code recording

GDDM graphics data display manager; graphics design data manager

GDMS Generalized Data Management System

GDO grid dip oscillator

GDS Graphic Data System

GE greater than

GEM graphics environment manager

GEMS General Educational Management System

gen generator

GENESYS General Engineering System

GERM generalized entity-relationship model

GERT Graphic Evaluation Review Technique

GH Giga Hertz

GICL Graphics Language

GIDS Generalized Intelligent Decision System

GIGO garbage-in, garbage-out

GIOC general input/output controller

GIM Generalized Information Management Language

GINO graphical input-output

GIPS Ground Information Processing System

GIPSY General Information Processing System

GIRS Generalized Information Retrieval System

GIS Generalized Information System

GKS Graphic Kernal System

GLOBECOM Global Communications

GMAP General Macro Assembly Program

GMIS General Management Information System

GMISCA General Motors Information System and Communications Activity

GMT general machine test

gnd ground

GNP gross national product

GOCI general operator-computer interaction

GOR general operational requirement

GPA general purpose analysis

GPAC general purpose analog computer

GPC general purpose computer

GPD general purpose discipline

GPDC general purpose digital computer

GPDS General Purpose Display System

GPI general purpose interface

GPIB general purpose interface bus

GPI/O general purpose input/output

GPL General Purpose Language; Generalized Programming Language

GPLAN Generalized Database Planning System

GPLP general purpose linear programming

GPM general purpose macrogenerator

GPMS general purpose microprogram simulator

GPR general purpose register

GPSS general purpose systems simulator

gr group

GRABP generalized remote data access database

GRABPS Generalized Remote Data Access DataBase System

GRACE graphic arts composing equipment

GRID graphical interactive display

GRIPHOS General Retrieval and Information Processing for Humanities-oriented studies

grp group

GRS Generalized Retrieval System

GSAM Generalized Sequential Access Method

GSI grand scale integration

GSM generalized sequential machine

GSS Graphic Service System

GT game theory; greater than

GTO graphics test organizer

GUIDE guidance of users of integrated data processing equipment

GULP general utility library program

H

h hack (a computer code or system hacker); half-word; hardware; hexidecimal

HASP Houston Automatic SPOOLing Priority

hb handbook

H-B hexidecimal to binary

HC handling capacity; hard copy; hybrid computer

HCI host control interface

HD half duplex; high density

HDAM Hierarchical Direct Access Method

HDDS High-density Data System

hdg heading

HDL Hardware Description Language

HDLC high-level data link control

hdr header

HDX half-duplex transmission

HELP Health Education and Lifestyles Program

HEM hybrid electromagnetic wave

HEMT high electron mobility transistor

HEP heterogenerous element processor

HEX hexidecimal

HF high frequency

HFCS Honeywell Financial and Corporate Planning System

hh hours

hh/mm hours/minutes

HICLASS Hughes Integrated Classification System

HIDAM Hierarchial Indexed Direct Access Method

HINIL high-noise immunity logic

HIO halt input/output

HIPAC Hitachi Parametron Automatic Computer

HIPO hierarchy plus input-process output

HIS Hospital Information Systems

HITS hobbyist's interchange tape standard

HLDLC high-level data link control

HLL High-Level Language

HMOS high speed metal oxide semiconductor

HNIL high-noise immunity logic

HOL High-Order Language

HOP Hybrid Operating System

HPF highest priority first

HPIB Hewlett-Packard Interface Bus

HPM Harvard Project Manager

HRM human resources management

HRS human resources

hs handset

HSAC high speed analog computer

HSAM Hierarchical Sequential Access Method

HSDA high speed data acquisition

HSM hierarchical storage manager; high speed memory

HSO hierarchical sequential organization

HSP high speed printers; high speed scientific processor

HSR high speed reader

HT horizontal tabulation

HTL   high threshold logic

HTTL   high power transistor-transistor logic

HUSAT   human sciences and advance technology

HV   high voltage

HVPS   high voltage power supply

HYCOTRAN   hybrid computer translator

HYSNC   horizontal synchronization

hz   hertz

I

i   indicator; input; interval; inverter

IA5   International Alphabet Number Five

IAG   interactive application generator

IAL   International Algebraic Language; International Algorithmic Language

IAP   integrated array processor

IAR   initial address register

IAS   immediate access storage; Institute for Advanced Study

IBA   Independent Broadcast Authority

IBG   interblock gap

IBM-PC   IBM personal computer

IBX   Integrated Business Exchange

IC   information center; input circuit; instruction counter; integrated circuits; interface control; interruption code

I&C   installation and checkout

ICA   integrated communications adapter

ICE   in-circuit emulation; input checking equipment

ICES   Integrated Civil Engineering System

ICF   integrated catalog facility; inter-communication flip-flop

ICG   interactive computer graphics

ICL   incoming line; Input Command Language

ICMS   Information Center Management System

IC/T   integrated computer/telemetry

IDA   interconnect device arrangement

IDAPS   Image Data Processing System

IDC   interactive datacomm configuration

IDCS   Instrumentation/Data Collection System; Integrated Document Control System

IDD   integrated data dictionary; International Direct Dial

IDDD   International Direct Distance Dialing

IDDS   International Digital Data Service

IDE   intelligent distributed editor

IDF   integrated data file

IDI   improved data interchange; intelligent dual interface

IDM   intelligent database machine

IDP   industrial data processing; integrated data processing

IDS   input data strobe; integrated data store

IE   information expert

IEO   integrated electronic office

IF   intermediate frequency

i/f   interface

IFAM   inverted file access mechanism

IFB   invitation for bid

IFPS   Interactive Financial Planning System

IFR   internal function register

IFRU   interference rejection unit

IGS   Integrated Graphics System

IH   interrupt handler

IIL   integrated injection logic

IIP   ISAM Interface Program

ILC   instruction length code; intelligent local-area network controller

ILLIAC   Illinois Automatic Computer

ILSW   interrupt level status word

IM   interface multiplexer

im   instrumentation

IMC   image motion compensation

imd   immediate

IM/DM   information management/data management

IMF interactive mainframe facility

IM/IPF information management/information processing family

IMIS Integrated Management Information System

IMM intelligent memory manager

IMNET International Marketing Network

IMP interface message processor

IMPRS Information Management Process Reporting System

IMS Information Management System; Instructional Management System; inventory management and simulator

IMT information management technology

IMTS Improved Mobile Telephone Service

IM/VE information management/virtual environment

IM/ZEUS Information Management/Zero Effort User System

in input

ind indicator

inf information

INFO information network and file organization

INFONET Information Network

init initiate; initialize

inq inquire

INS International Navigation System

inst instruction

int interger; initial; interrupt

INTCON international connection

I/O input/output

IOB input/output buffer

IOC input/output controller; input/output converter; input/output control center; input/output control command; Input/Output Control Services; Input/Output Control System

I/OM input/output multiplexer

IOO input/output operation

IOP input/output processor

IOPS Input/Output Programming System

IOR input/output register

IOREQ input/output request

IORL Input/Output Requirements Language

IOS Integrated Office System

IOT image output terminals; input/output transfer

IOTA information overload testing apparatus

IOU immediate operation use

IP information processing; instruction processor; internet protocol; item processing

IPA intermediate power amplifier

IPB intermediate parts breakdown

IPC industrial process control; industrial programmable control; information processing center; Internet packet controller

IPD insertion phase delay

IPE interpret parity error

IPF interactive productivity facility

IPL initial program loader

IPL-V Information Processing Language V

IPM identical phase modulation; impulses per minute

IPN Information Processing Network; inspection progress notifications; instant private network

IPO input/process/output

IPOT inductive potential divider

IPS inches per second

IQF interactive query facility

IR information retrieval; instruction register

IRC international record carrier

IRD international resource development

IRDB information retrieval data bank

IRG inter-record gap

IRP initial receiving point

IRR internal rate of return

IRS Information Retrieval System

IS indexed sequential; information systems; international standard; interval signal

ISA interrupt storage area

ISAM indexed sequential access method; integrated switching and multiplexing

ISBN International Standard Book Number

ISC inter-systems coupling

IS&D integrate sample and dump

ISDN Integrated Services Digital Network

ISDOS Information System Design and Optimization System

ISI internally specified index

ISK insert storage key

ISL Information System Language; Instructional Systems Language; Interactive Simulation Language

ISM industrial, scientific, and medical equipment; integrated service management

ISN Information Systems Network

ISO individual system operation

ISODATA Iterative Self-Organizing Data Analysis Technique

ISP information systems planning; instruction set processor

ISPL Instruction Set Processor Language

ISPN international standard program number

ISPS instruction set processor specifications

ISR infomation and systems research; information storage and retrieval; intersecting storage rings

IST international security technology

IT information technology; input translator; intelligent terminal; internal translator; item transfer

ITDM intelligent time-division multiplexer

ITE integrated terminal equipment

ITS invitation to send

IUP installed user program

iv inverter

IVDT integrated voice/data terminal

IW index word

ix index; interactive executive

J

JA jump address

JAD joint application design

JCL Job Control Language

JCP job control procedure

jctn junction

JDC job description card

JES job entry subsystem

JGN junction gate number

JIB job information block

JIP joint input processing

JIS Japanese industrial standard

JIT just-in-time

JO job order

JOBCAT job catalog

JOC joint operations center

JOD journal of development

JPW job processing word

j/s justified

JT job table

JUG Joint Users Group

K

k kilobyte

KAK key-auto-key

KAU keystation adapter unit

kb kilobyte; keyboard

kbps kilobits per second

KCC keyboard common contact

KCS thousand characters per second

KDR keyboard data recorder

KDS keyboard display station; Key Display System; Kiting Detection System

KEE knowledge engineering environment

KEEPS KODAK Ektaprint Electronic Publishing System

kHz kilohertz

KIMS KODAK Image Management System

KISS   keep it simple, sir
KL   key length
KMS   keysort multiple selectors
KP   key pulsing
KPC   keyboard priority controller
KPR   Kodak photo resist
KSAM   Keyed Sequential Access Method

KSDS   key sequence data set
KSR   keyboard send-receive set
KST   known segment table
KTR   keyboard typing reperforator
KWIC   key word in context
KWOC   key word out of context

L

l   label; level; line; load
LAC   load accumulator
LACM   load accumulator with magnitude
LADT   local area data transport
LALR   look ahead
LAMA   local automatic message accounting
LAN   local area network
LAP   link access protocol
LARC   Livermore Automatic Research Computer
LARCT   last radio contact
laser   Light Amplification by Stimulated Emission of Radiation
LATA   local access transport area
LB   line buffer
LBA   linear bound automation
lbl   label
LC   last card; level control; line connector; lower case
LCB   line control block
LCD   line curent disconnect; liquid crystal display
LCDTL   load-compensated diode-transistor logic
LCL   Linkage Control Language
lcl   local
LCM   least common multiple
LCP   Language Conversion Program
LCR   least-cost routing; local storage
lczr   localizer
LD   linear decision; logic driver; long distance
ld   load
LDA   locate drum address
LDC   latitude data computer
LDDS   Low Density Data System

LDE   linear differential equations
LDM   limited-distance modem
LDRI   low data rate input
LDS   large disk storage
LDT   logic design transistor; long distance transmission
LDX   long distance xerography
LE   leading edge; less than or equal to
LEAS   lower echelon automatic switchboard
LED   light emitting diode
LEO   Lyons Electronic Office (an early computer)
LET   logical equipment table
LEXIS®   Computerized legal database of Mead Data Central
LEXPAT®   computerized legal patent information database of Mead Data Central
LF   line feed; logical file; low frequency
LG   line generator
LGN   line gate number
lgnt   length
LIC   linear integrated circuit
LICOF   land lines communication facilities
LIFO   last in, first out
LIM   line interface module
lim   limit
LIMAC   Large Integrated Monolithic Array Computer
LINAC.   linear accelerator
LINC   laboratory instrument computer
LINEII   Logic and Information Network Compiler II
LIOCS   Logical Input/Output Control System
LISP   list processing

lit   literal
LIU   line interface unit
LL   loudness level; low level
LLL   low level logic
L/MF   low and medium frequency
LMLR   load memory lockout register
lmt   limit
LO   line occupancy; local oscillator; low order
LOCS   logic and control simulator
log   logarithm; logic
LOGANDS   logical commands
LOGI   logarithm computing instrument
LOGRAM   logical program
LOMAS   Law Office Management and Accounting System
LOS   loss of signal
LOT   linear quantizer
LP   linear programming; line printer
LPM   lines per minute
LPS   lines per second
LPSW   load program status word
LQ   letter quality
LQP   letter quality printer
LR   level recorder; line relay; logical record
LRA   load real address
LRC   longitudinal redundancy check
LRD   long range data
LRECL   logical record length
LRIM   long range input monitor

LRS   long range search
LRU   least recently used
LS   language specification; laser system; low speed
LSA   local system administrator; logistics systems architecture
LSB   least significant bit
LSD   least significant digit; line sharing device;.line signal detector
LSI   large scale integration
LSNLIS   Linear Sciences Natural Language Information System
LSO   local storage option
LSP   low speed printer
LSSGR   local switching system general requirements
LSTTL   low-power schottky transistor-transistor logic
LT   less than; logic theorist
ltl   literal
ltr   letter
LTRS   letters shift
LU   logical unit
LUB   logical unit block
LUT   local user terminal
LV   low voltage
LVCD   least voltage coincidence detection
LWD   larger word
lwr   lower

M

m   magnetic; media; mega; meter; milli-monitor
MA   memory address; message assembler; modify address
MAC   machine-aided cognition; multi-access computing
MACE   Management Access in a Computer Environment
macro   macroinstruction
MACS   Management and Computer Systems; Multiline Automatic Calling System
MACSYSMA   MACs Symbolic Manipulation

MACU   multidrop auto-call unit
MAD   Michigan Algorithmic Decoder; multiaperture device; multiple access device
MADT   microalloy diffused-base transistor
mag   magnetic
MAGCARD   Magnetic Card Word Processor (IBM)
MAL   Macro Assembly Language
MAM   multiple access to memory
MAN   Metropolitan Area Network
man   manual
MANOP   manual of operation

MAP macro arithmetic processor; memory allocation and protection; message acceptance pulse; manufacturing automation protocol

MAPICS Manufacturing and Accounting Production Information Construction System

MAPS Management Analysis and Planning Software

MAR memory address register

MARC machine-readable cataloging

MARS memory address register storage; Multi-access Airline Reservation System

MARTEC martin thin-film electronic circuit

MAS Management Advisory Services

MASS Monitor and Assembly System; multiple access sequential selection

MAT microalloy transistor

max maximum

MB memory buffer

mb megabyte

M-B make-break

MBB make before break

MBPS megabits per second

MBQ modified biquinary code

MBR memory buffer register

MBR-E memory buffer register, even

MBR-O memory buffer register, odd

MBT memory block table

MC magnetic core; manual control; master control; memory controller

MC megacycle

MCC management control center; master communications center; multi component circuits

MCD master clerical data

MCM magnetic core memory

MCP Master Control Program

MCP/AS Master Control Program/Advanced System

MCR magnetic character reader; magnetic character recognition; master control routine

MCS Master Control System; Multi-programmed Computer System; multi-purpose communications and signaling

MCS-A Multi-Functional Communications System — Asynchronous

MSCP mass storage control protocol

MCU master control unit; micro-program control unit; multiple control unit

MCW modulated continuous wage

MCX minimum cost estimating

MD magnetic disk; main drum; message data; monitor display; motor drive; multiple data (stream); multiple dissemination

M-D modulation-demodulation

MDC modification detection code

MDI Mobil Data International, Incorporated

MDM modular data module

MDR multi channel data recorder; memory data register

MDS Malfunction Detection System; Market Decision System; Memory Disk System; Microprocessor Development System; minimum discernable signal; Modern Data Systems; Multiple Data-set System

MDSB message digest signature block

MDT mean down time

ME mechanical efficiency; modular electronics

me microelectronic

MEDLARS Medical Literature Analysis and Retrieval System

MEDLINE Medlars On-line System

mega million

mem memory

MEMISTOR memory resistor storage device

MER minimum energy requirements

MES miscellaneous equipment specifications

MetFACS Metropolitan Life Insurance Company Financial and Administrative Customer Services System

MEW microwave early warning

MEX military exchange

MF main frame; medium frequency

mf microfiche

MFC magnetic-tape field scan; micro-functional circuit

MFCM multi-function card machine

MFKP multifrequency key pulsing

MFLOPS million floating point instructions per second

MFM modified frequency modulation

MFS magnetic tape field search; message format services

MFSK multiple frequency shift keying

MFT Multiprogramming with a Fixed Number of Tasks

MG motor generator

mgmt management

mgr manager

MHD moving-head disk

MHP message handling processor

MHz megahertz

MI manual input; mode indicator; multiple instruction (stream)

MIACS Manufacturing Information and Control System

MIC magnetic ink characters; microwave integrated circuit

MICA macro instruction compiler assembler

MICR magnetic-ink character-recognition

micro microcomputer

MICS Management Information and Control System

MIDAC Michigan digital automatic computer

MIMD multiple-instruction stream, multiple data stream

MIMR magnetic ink mark recognition

min minimum; minute

MINX Multimedia Information Network Exchange

MIO multiple input-output stream

MIP manual input processing

MIPE modular information processing equipment

MIPS million instructions per second

MIR memory information register; memory input register

MIS Management Information Systems; marketing information system

MISD multiple-instruction stream, single-data stream

MISP Medical Information System Programs

MIT master instruction tape

MIU machine interface unit; multistation interface unit

MKS meter-kilogram-second

ML machine language

MLA microprocessor language assembler

MLB multilayer board

MLE microprocessor language editor

MLPWB multilayer printed wiring board

MLR memory lockout register

MM main memory

mm millimeter

MMA multiple module access

MMD moving map display

mmddyy month, day, year

MMS mass memory store; municipal management system

MNCS multipoint network-control system

MO manual output; master oscillator; miscellaneous operation

M&O maintenance and operations

MOC master operational computer

mod modular; modulation; module

MODEM modulator-demodulator

MOE meaure of effectiveness

MOHILL Machine Oriented High Level Language

MOL machine oriented language

mon monitor

MONOS monitor out of service

MOPA master oscillator-power amplifier

MOPB manually operated plotting board

MOS management operating system; metal oxide semiconductor

MP maintenance point; mathematical programming; modem port

mp multi-processor

MPACS Management Planning and Control System

MPCC multiprotocol communications controller

MPDA monitor printer diskette adaptor

MPG microwave pulse generator

MPL multischedule private line

mpl multiple

MP/M Multiprogramming Control Program

MPP mono power pack

MPPL Multi-purpose Processing Language

MPS Microprocessor System; Multiprogramming System

MPSX Mathematical Programming System Extended

MPU microprocessor unit

mpu multiplex

mpy multiply
MQ multiplier quotient
MQR multiplier quotient register
MR memory read; memory register
MRAD mass random access disk
MRD multi-region option
MRO maintenance, repair and operating; multi-region option
MRP manufacturing resources planning
MRPS Materials Requirement Planning System
MRT multiple requests terminal
MRU machine records unit
MS magnetic storage; memory system
ms manuscript
MSB most significant bit
MSD most significant digit
MS-DOS™ Microsoft™ Disk Operating System
msec millisecond
msg message
MSG/WTG message waiting
MSI medium scale integration
msk mask
MSNET Microsoft Network
MSOS Mass Storage Operating System
MSR management support representative
MSS Mass Storage System; Multi-lan Storage System
MSU modem sharing units
MSUDC Michigan State University Discrete Computer
MT machine translation; magnetic tape; maintenance technician; measured time; multiple transfer
MTBF mean-time-between-failure
MTC magnetic tape control

MTCU magnetic tape control unit
MTF mean time to failure
MTL merged transistor logic
MTM methods-time measurement
MTR magnetic tape recorder
MTS Magnetic Tape System; Message Telecommunications Services; Michigan Terminal System
MT/SC magnetic tape/selectric composer
MTSO Mobil Telephone Switching Office
MT/ST magnetic tape selectric typewriter
MTT magnetic tape terminal; magnetic tape transport
MTTF mean time to failure
MTTR mean time to repair
MTU magnetic tape unit; multiplexer and terminal unit
MUL Multiplexed Information and Computing System
MULTICS Multiplexed Information and Computing Service
MUMPS Massachusetts General Hospital Utility Multi-Programming System
mux multiplexer; multiplexing
MV mean value; measured value
mv millivolt
MVDI microfield virtual device interface
MVS multiple virtual storage; multiprogramming with virtual storage
MVT multiprogramming with variable number of tasks
MW memory write
MWI message waiting indicator
mx matrix; multiplex

N

n nano; no; number; numeric
NA not assigned
NAARS National Automated Accounting Research System
NAK negative acknowledgment
NAND negated and
NAPLPS North American presentation-level-protocol syntax

NAU network addressable unit
NBCD natural binary coded decimal
NBFM narrow band frequency modulation
NC network connect; no connection; no change; no charge; numerical control
NCC network control computer

NCCF network communications control facility

NCP Network Control Program

NCR-DNA NCR Corporation Distributed Network Architecture

NCS National Communications Systems

NCTE network channel terminating equipment

NDR nondestructive read

NDRO nondestructive readout

NDT net data throughput; nondestructive testing

NEC National Electrical Code

neg negative

NELIAC Navy Electronics Laboratory International Algol Compiler

NEP never ending program

NES not elsewhere specified

NETDA Network Design and Analysis

NEXIS® Computerized database of news, business, etc. of Mead Data Central

NEXT near end crosstalk loss

NFS Network Facilities Services; Network File System

NI numerical index

NIC network interface controller

NIFTP Network Independent File Transfer Program

nil nothing

NIOS Nixdorf Integrated Office System

NIPO negative input, positive output

NIU network interface unit

NJE network job entry

NLP nonlinear programming

NLQ near letter quality

NLR noise load ratio

NMC network management center

NME noise measuring equipment

NMI non-maskable interrupt

NMOS m-channel metal-oxide semiconductor

nom nominal

NoOp no operation

NOP no operation

NORC naval ordnance research computer

NOS/VE Network Operating System/ Virtual Environment

NP net proceeds; nondeterministic polynomial

NP/L New Program Language

NPDA network problem determination aid

NPEF new product evaluation form

NPL Natural Processing Language; new product line

NPSI network control program packet switching interface

NPV net present value

NR noise ratio; not required

nr number

NRC noise reduction coefficient

NRFD not ready for data

NRT non-requesting terminal

NRZ non-return to zero

NRZ1 non-return to zero one

NS national standard

ns nanoseconds

NSC noise suppression circuit

nsec nanosecond

NSN national stock numbers

NSP network services protocol

NT no transmission; not tested

NTN National Telecommunications Network

NTO network terminal option

NTPF number of terminals per failure

NTS Network Test System

NTSC National Television Standard Code

num number

NVM nonvolatile memory

O

o octal; output

OA office assistant; operations analysis; office automation

OAG EE Official Airline Guide Electronic Edition

OAS Office Automation System

OASF Office Automation System Facility

OB output buffer

O-B octal to binary

OBR optical bar code

O/C open circuit

O&C operations and checkout

OCC operations control center

OCO object code only

OCP optical character printing

OCR optical character reader; optical character recognition

oct octal

OCTOPUS Network of Control Data Corporation

OD output data

O-D octal to decimal

OD³ optical digital data disk

ODA office document architecture

ODE on-line data entry; ordinary differential equation

ODIF office document interchange format

ODS Office Dialog System

OEM original equipment manufacturer

ofc office

off office

oh off hook

OIS Office Information System (WANG)

OJT on-the-job training

ol on-line

o/l on-line

OLC on-line computer

OLM on-line monitor

OLPS On-line Programming System

OLRT on-line real time

OLTP on-line terminal processing

OM operations maintenance

O&M organizations and methods

OMR optical mark reader

OMS office management system

OP office products

op operation; output

OPEN Open Protocol Enhanced Networks

OPM operations per minute; operator programming method

opn open

opnd operand

opt optical

OPTUL Optical Pulse Transmitter Using Laser

OR operational research; operations research; optical reader

O/R on request

ORCA on-line resource control aid

ORDVAC ordnance variable automatic computer

org organization

orig origination

OS Operating System

OSA open system architecture

OSAM Overflow Sequential Access Method

OSAR optical storage and retrieval

OSF office systems family

OSI on-line software; open systems interconnection

OS/MFT Operating System/Multiprogramming with a Fixed Number of Tasks

OS/MVS Operating System/Multiprogramming with Virtual Storage

OS/MVT Operating System/Multiprogramming with a Variable Number of Tasks

OSR optical scanning recognition

OSWS operating system work station

ot overtime

out output

ovflo overflow

P

p packed; parity; power; punch

PA paper advance; power amplifier; program access; program analysis; public address

PABX private automated branch exchange

PACEO Professional Application Creation Environment

PACT pay actual computer time; Production Analysis Control Technique

PAD packet assembler/disassembler

PAL Programmable Algorithm Machine Assembly Language; programmable array logic

PAM personal accounting management; pulse amplitude modulation

par parameter

para paragraph

PARS Programmed Airline Reservation System

PAS Personal Accounting System

PAT printer action table

patn pattern

PAX private automatic exchange

PB pay-back period; plug board

P-BIT parity bit

PBX private branch exchange; paper change; personal computer; printed circuit; process control; professional computer; program counter; punched card

P-C process controller

PCA physical configuration audit

PCB printed circuit board

PCC program-controlled computer

PCDC punched card data processing

PC-DOS Personal Computer Disk Operating System

PICS Personal Computer Instructional System

PC/IX Personal Computer/Interactive Executive

PCM plug-compatible machine; plug-compatible mainframe; pulse-code modulation

PCNP Personal Computer Network Program

PCP Primary Control Program

PCR program control register

PCS Personal Computer System; program control sheet; Punched card system

PC/T personal computer/technology

PDA pushdown automation

PDE partial differential equation

PDL Program Design Language

PDP programmed data processor

PDR preliminary data report; processing data rate

PDS personal decision series; Problem Descriptor System; professional development seminar

PE project engineer

PEER project engineer evaluation report

pem photoelectromagnetic

PEN Purchasing Electronic Notebook

PERCOS Performance Coding System

PERT Program Evaluation and Review Technique

PES photoelectric scanning

PET Personal Electronic Translator

PF page formatter; program function

PFET programmable front-end processor

PFK program function key

PF1 program function key number one

(*"PF" followed by a number usually indicates a program function key on a computer terminal keyboard. There are often several of these, numbered "PF1" to "PF9", for example. The same is true for "F" which stands for "function key" and is often seen as "F1," "F2," "F3," etc.*)

PFR power-fail recovery; power-fail restart

PGC professional graphics controller

PGS Program Generation System

PHIGS Programmers Hierarchical Interactive Graphics System

PHIL Programmable Algorithm Machine High Level Language

pht phototube

PI performance index; profitability index: programmed instruction

PIA peripheral interface adaptor

PIC priority interrupt controller

PICO power integrity corporation

PICU priority interrupt control unit

PIN personal identification number; police information network

PINO positive input, negative output

PIP paper impact printing; programmable integrated processor

PISO parallel in, serial out

PISW process interrupt status word

PIT programmable interval timer

PIU path information unit; plug-in unit

pkd packed

P&L profit and loss

PL Programmable Language

PLA programmable logic array

PLATO programmed logic for automatic teaching operation

PLDM power line disturbance monitor

PLL phase locked loop

PLM pulse length modulation

PL/M Programming Language M

PL/1 Programming Language One

PLT program library tape

PM phase modulation; preventative maintenance; procedures manual

PMC pseudo machine code

PMOS positive metal-oxide semiconductor

PMS Personal Mailing System; processor memory switch; Program Management System; Project Management System; Public Message System

PMT page map table

PMTA page map table address register

PMX packet multiplexer

PND present next digit

PNX private network exchange

PO purchase order

po partitioned

POGO programmer oriented graphics operation

POL Problem-Oriented Language; Procedure-Oriented Language; Process Oriented Language

PORT photo-optical recorder tracker

POS point-of-sale; Primary Operating System; positive

POSET partially ordered set

POT physical organization table

PP peripheral processor

pp pages; preprocessor

PPL Polymorphic Programming Language; preferred products list

PPM pulses per minute

PPMS Professional Productivity Management System

PPS Parallel Processing System; pulses per second

PPT punched paper tape

PPU peripheral processing unit

PR pattern recognition; physical records

pr print

prelim preliminary

PRIM Programmed Instruction for Management Education

PRISM Programmed Integrated System Maintenance

PRM preventative maintenance

prm primary

proc procedure; processor

prof profession

PROFIT Programmed Reviewing, Ordering and Forecasting Inventory Technique

PROFS Professional Office System

prog program; programming

PROM programmable read only memory

PRR pulse repetition rate

PRS Pattern Recognition System

PRT portable remote terminal; production run tape; program reference table

prt printer

PRTM printing response time monitor

prty priority

PS physical sequential; power supply; pico-seconds

PSA personal statement analyzer; push-down stack automation

PSE packet switching exchange

psec picosecond

PSK phase shift keying

PSL/PSA Problem Statement Language/Problem Specification Analyzer

PSOS Provably Secure Operating System

PSR program support representative

PSS Public Safety System

PSU program storage unit

PSW program status word

PT paper tape; part time; program table; punched tape

PTF program temporary fix

PTP paper tape punch

PTR paper tape reader

PTT postal telephone and telegraph

PU power unit; processing unit

PUB physical unit block

PUC Public Utilities Commission

PUFFT Purdue University Fast FORTRAN·Compiler

PV present value

PWB printer wire board

PWI power indicator

PWM pulse width modulation

PWS programmer work station**

Q

QA   quality assurance
QAM   quadrature amplitude modulation
QCC   quality control circles
QF   quality factor
QIC   quarter-inch cartridge
QIL   quad-inline
QISAM   Queued Indexed Sequential Access Method
QIT   Quality Information and Test System
QL   Query Language
QMF   query management facility

QMS   Quality Micro Systems
QPL   qualified products list
QSAM   queued sequential access method
QT   queueing theory
QTAM   Queued Teleprocessing Access Method
qty   quantity
QUIP   quere interactive processor
QUIP   quad in-line package
QWERTY   standard typewriter keyboard, stands for second row left, first six letters: q/w/e/r/t/y

R

r   read; reader; request; right
RACE   random access computer equipment; rapid automatic checkout equipment
RACF   resource access control facility
RAD   random access data; random access drive; rapid access disk
RADAR   radio detection and ranging
RADAS   random access discrete address
RAI   random access and inquiry
RAIR   random access information retrieval
RALU   register-equipped arithmetic logic unit
RAM   random access memory
RAMAC   random access; Random Access Method for Accounting and Control
RAMIS   Rapid Access Management Information System
RAMPS   resource allocation in multi-project scheduling
RAMS   Record Archival Management System
RAS   Remote Access System; Resource Analysis System; row address strobe
RAYDAC   ratheon digital automatic computer

RBA   relative byte address
RBMS   Remote Bridge Management Software
RBOC   Regional Bell Operating Companies
RC   resistance-capacitance, resistor-capacitor; radio-controlled; resistance coupled
RCAC   Remote Computer Access Communications Service
RCC   radio common carrier
RCD   receiver-carrier detector
RCTL   resister-capacitor-transistor logic
rcv   receive
rcvr   receiver
rd   read
R&D   research and development
RDC   remote data connector
RDE   received data enable
RDF   record definition field
RDOS   Real-time Disk Operating System
rdr   reader
rdy   ready
R&E   research and engineering
rec   record
RECFM   record format

ref reference
reg register
ReGIS remote graphics instruction set
rel release
rem remainder
REMIS Real Estate Management Information System
REMOS Resources Management On-line System
REQUEST Restricted English Question-Answering
rew rewind
RF radio frequency; revisable-form
RFD ready for data
RFI radio-frequency interference; report/file language; request for information
RFMS Remote File Management System
RFQ request for quote
RGB red-green-blue (color monitor)
RGP remote graphics processor
RH report heading
RI read in; reliability index; ring indicator
RIM read in mode
RISC reduced instruction set computer
RJE remote job entry
RL relocation library
RLD relocation dictionary
RLIN Research Libraries Information Network
RLSD received line signal detector
RM records management; record mark
RMM read mostly memory
RMN Remote Microphone Network
RMS root mean square
RMU retention memory unit
RMW read—modify—write
RO read only; read out; receive only
ROBIN Remote On-line Business Information Network
ROCR remote optical character recognition
ROI return on investment
ROIT return on investment time
ROM read-only memory
ROS read-only storage; Resident Operating System
ROTR receive only typing reperforation
RPC register protective circuitry

RPG register program generator
RPG II Report Program Generator Second Version
RPG III Report Program Generator Third Version
RPQ request for price quotation
RPROM reprogrammable read only memory
RPS rotational position sensing
rpt report
RR register to register instruction; remove and replace
RRDS relative record data set
RS recommended standard; remote station; reset key
R-S reset—set
RSCS Remote SPOOLing Communication Subsystem
RSL Requirements Specification Language
RSM Resource Management System
RSP remote switching partition
RSS Remote Speaking System; Resource Security System
RS232 Recommended Standard Interface Number 232
RT read tape; real time; register transfer; remote terminal
R&T research and technology
RTB read tape binary
RTBM real-time bit mapping
RTC real-time command; relative time clock
RTCC real-time computer complex
RTCF real-time computer facility
RTCS Real-time Computer System
RTCU real-time control unit
RTD real-time display
RTDHS Real-time Data Handling System
RTE real-time execution
RT/IOC real-time input/output controller
RTIS Real-time Information Retrieval System
RTL Real-time Language; resistor-transistor logic
RTM real-time monitor; register transfer module
RTMOS Real-time Multiprogramming Operating System
RTOS Real-time Operating System

RTS request to send
RU request/response unit
RW read-write

R/W read/write
RWM read-write memory
RXD received data

S

s second; sequential; sign; switch
SAC Scriptomatic Addressing Computer; store and clear accumulator
SAD serial analog delay
SADF semi-automatic document feeder
SAH standard allowed hours; standard average hour
SAKI Self-organizing Automatic Keyboard Instructor
SAL Symbolic Assembly Language; Systems Assembly Language
SAM secure access multiport; sequential access method; sort and merge; system activity monitor
SAP Symbolic Assembly Program
SAS Statistical Analysis System
SAU secure access unit
SBC signal board computer; small business computer
SBI synchronous bus interface
SBN Standard Book Number
SBS Satellite Business System
SCC satellite communications controller; specialized common carrier; storage connecting circuit
SCL system communication location
SCM segment control module; small core memory
SCP Systems Control Program
SCPC single channel per carrier
SCR silicon controlled rectifier
SCS Service Card System; Small Computer System
SCSI Samll Computer System Interface
SCT subroutine call table
SCTO soft carrier turn off
SDA screen design aid; source data automation
SDE software development environment
SDF screen definition facility
SDI selective dissemination of information; source data information; super data interchange
SDLC synchronous data link control
SDRM sub-rate time-division multiplexer
SDM systems design methodology; systems development methodology
SDS Scientific Data Systems
SDT source data terminal
SE service engineer; system extension
SEAC Standards Eastern Automatic Computer
sec second
sect section
seg segment
sel select
seq sequence
SEQUEL Structured English Query Language
serv service
SEU source entry utility
S&F store and forward
SFD symbolic file directory
SGND signal ground
SH switch hook
SI shift in; International System of Units
SID swift interface device
SIE start interpretive execution
sig signal
SIM signal interface module
sim simulation
SIMD single-instruction stream, multiple-data stream
SIMP satellite information message protocol
SIMULA Simulation Language
SIO serial input/output
SIP simulated input processor; Single In-line Package; Symbolic Input Program
SIPO serial in, parallel out

SIR selective information retrieval; statistical information retrieval

SISD single-instruction stream, single-data stream

SISO serial in, serial out

SJF shortest job first

SL storage location

SLAM Simulation Language for Alternative Modeling

SLR simple left-to-right

SLSI super large scale integration

SLT solid logic technology

SM shared memory

SMART System Management and Review Technique; System Monitoring and Reporting Tool

SMD scheduling management display

SMDR station message detail recording

SMF systems management facilities

SMRT signal message rate timing

SMT segment table map

SMTE segment table map entry

SN switching network

SNA systems network architecture

SNAP systems network access protocol

SNF shared network facilities; shared network facilities agreements

SNOBOL String Oriented Symbolic Language

SNR signal/noise radio

SO serial output; shift-out

SOA state of the art

SOAP Symbolic Optimizer and Assembly Program

SOB start of block

SODA system optimization and design algorithm

SOH start of header

SOM start of message; self organizing machine

SOP standard operating procedure; study organization plan

SOR successive overrelaxation

SOS Share Operating System; silicon-on-sapphire; Symbolic Operating System

SP single purpose; space character; start point; structured programming

SPC stored program control; stored programmed command; system professional computer

spec specification

spkr speaker

SPL Simple Programming Language

SPM set program mask

SPOC Space Shuttle on Board Personal Computer

SPOOL Simultaneous Peripheral Operation On-Line

SPQC Statistical Process and Quality Control

SPS stand-by power source; Symbolic Programming System

SQA software quality assurance

SQC statistical quality control

SQD signal quality detector

SQL Structured Query Language

SQUARE Specifying Queries as Relational Expressions

SQUID Superconducting Quantum Interference Device

SR status register

S-R set–reset

s/r subroutine

SRFT shortest remaining time first

SRL system reference library

SROS Seybold Report on Office Systems

SRT single request terminal

SS solid state; storage to storage instruction

SSB single sideband

SSD solid state storage device

SSDA synchronous serial data adapter

SS/DD single-sided/double-density

SSEC selective sequence electronic calculator

SSI small-scale integration

SSL solid statement library

SSM set system mask

SSP Scientific Subroutine Package

SSR solid state relay

SS/SD single-sided/single-density

ST segment table; standard time; system test

st start

STAM shared tape allocation manager

STAR self testing and repair; status application resource

STC standard transmission code

std standard

STDM synchronous time division multiplexer; synchronous time-division multiplexing

STE standard terminal equipment

STED Specified Technique for Efficient Typesetting

STI scientific and technical information

STM system master tape

stor storage

STORM Statistically Oriented Matrix Program

STP selective tape print; system test procedure; System Training Program

STR segment table register; synchronous transmit receive

STRESS Structural Engineering Systems Solver

STRUDL Structural Design Language

STS Shared Tenant Services

STTL standard transistor-transistor logic

STX start of text

SU signalling unit; storage unit

sub subtract

SURF system utilization reporting facility

SVC supervisor call; switched virtual circuit

SVD simultaneous voice/data

SW status word

SWAC Standards Western Automatic Computer

SYLK symbolic link

syn synchronous

sync synchronize

SYSGEN system generation

SYSLIB system library

SYSLOG system logic

SYSOPS system operators

SYSOUT system out

T

t terminal; time

TA training analyst

TAC Telenet Access Controller

TADI time assigned data interpolation

TADS Teletypewriter Automatic Dispatch System; Test and Debug System

TAOS Transportation's Automated Office System

TAS telephone answering service

TASI time assigned speech interpolation

TAT turn-around-time

TAXIR taxonomic information retrieval

tbl table

TBM terabit memory

TBMT transmitter buffer empty

TC tactical computer; terminal computer; terminal controller; transfer control; transmission control

TCAM Telecommunications Access Method

TCDMS Telecommunications/Data Management System

TCM thermal conduction module

TCP Tatpe Conversion Program; transmitter clock

TCPC tab card punch control

TCP/IP Transmission Control Protocol/Internet Protocol

TCS Terminal Control System

TCU transmission control unit; tape control unit

TD tabular data; transmitted data

TDM text and date messaging; time-division multiplexer

TDMA time-division multiple access

T/DOS Tape/Disk Operating System

TDR transmit data register

TE test equipment

T&E test and evaluation

tech technology

TELCO telephone company

TELEX Teleprinter Exchange Service

TELENET® Network of General Telephone and Electronics Company

temp temporary

TESS Total Engineering Support System

THE SOURCEsm Source Telecomputing Network

3M computer workstation of one megabyte random access memory, one megapixel resolution, and over one million instructions per second

TI   type in

TICCIT   Time-shared Interactive Computer-controlled Informational Television

TIES   Total Integrated Engineering System

TIF   The Information Facility

TIO   test input/output

TIP   technical information processing; terminal interface message processor; total information processing

TIPC   Texas Instruments personal computer

TIPS   Text Information Processing System

TIS   Total Information System

TIU   tape identification unit

TL   tape library

TLB   translation lookaside buffer

TLU   table look up

TM   tape mark

TMA   telephone management and accounting

TMCC   time-multiplexed communication channel

TMP   thermo magnetic printing

TMR   triple modular redundancy

TMS   telecommunications message switcher; Telephone Management System

TMU   time measurement unit; transmission measurement unit

TNS   Transaction Network Service

TOC   table of contents

TOD   time-of-day

TODS   Transactions on Database Systems

TOE   total operating expense

TOMS   Transactions on Mathematical Software

TOP   technology office protocol

TOPLAS   Transactions on Programming Languages and Systems

TOS   Tape Operating System; Terminal Oriented Software; Terminal Oriented System

TOSS   Total Office Support System

cessing; test procedure; transaction processing

tp   tape

TPF   transaction processing facility

TPI   tracks per inch

tpr   teleprinter

TPU   tape preparation unit

TR   tape recorder

TRAC   Texas reconfigurable array computer

TRACS   Teleprocessing Remote Access Control System

TRAP™   Tandem Recursive Algorithm Process

TRC   telephone relay coupler

trn   transfer

TROLL   (Computer language for testing, using linear and nonlinear equations)

TS   temporary storage

T/S   time sharing

TSDM   Time-shared Data Management System

TSDOS   Time-shared Disk Operating System

TSM   Time-shared Monitor System

TSO   time-sharing option

TSO/E   time-sharing option extensions

TSOS   Time-sharing Operating System

TSS   task state segment; Time-shared System

tt   teletypewriter

TTC   tape to card

TTL   transistor-to-transistor logic

TTP   tape to print

TTTL   transistor-to-transistor-to-transistor logic

tty   teletypewriter

TU   tape unit

TUC   terminal usage charge

TUT   transistor under test

TVT   television typewriter terminal

t/w   typewriter

TWT   travelling wave tube

TWX   Teletypewriter Exchange Service

tx   transmit

TXD   transmit data

TYMNET   Timeshare Incorporated Network

U

u unit; utility
UADPS Uniform Automatic Data Processing System
UART universal asynchronous receiver/transmitter
UBC universal buffer controller
UC upper case
UCA user computed address
UCB unit control block
UCL user control list
UCS universal character set; Universal Classification System
UCW unit control word
UDC universal decimal classification
UDK user defined key
UDS Universal Data Systems
UHF ultra-high frequency
UIL Univac Interactive Language
UIM ultra-intelligent machine
ULA uncommitted logic array
UNINET® Network of United Telecom Company
UNIVAC universal automatic computer
UL1 User Language One

UP user program
UPC universal product code
UPL Universal Programming Language
UPS Uninterruptable Power Systems
UR unit record
US unit separator
USART universal synchronous/asynchronous receiver/transmitter
USAS Univac Standard Airline System
USASCII USA Standard Code for Information Interchange
USDA United States Department of Agriculture
USOC universal service ordering code
USRT universal synchronous receiver/transmitter
UT up time
ut utility
UTS Universal Timesharing System
UTS-M Universal Timesharing System for Mainframes
UTS-S Universal Timesharing System for Superminis
UTTC universal tape-to-tape converter
UUT unit under test

V

v video; virtual; voice; volt
VA video amplifier
VAB voice answer back
VAC value-added carrier
VAD value-added dealer
VAL Vicarm Arm Language
VAN Value-Added Network
VAR value-added remarketer; value-added reseller
var variable
VASD value-added systems distributor
VAT voice activated typewriter
VAU volume allocation unit
VAV Visicalc advanced version
VAX (A computer series of Digital Equipment Corporation); virtual

address extension
VC virtual circuit; Visicalc
VCNA VTAM Communications Network Application
VCR video cassette recorder
VCS View Control System
VDA/D video display adapter with digital enhancement
VDG video display generator
VDI virtual device interface
VDL Vienna Definition Language
VDT video display terminal; video display tube
VDU video display unit; visual display unit
V/F voltage to frequency converter

VFU vertical format unit
VHF very high frequency
VHM virtual hardware monitor
VHS video home system
VHSIC very high speed integrated circuit
VIC variable instruction computer
VIDAC virtual data acquisition and control; visual information display and control
VIDAT visual data acquisition
VIP variable information processing; visual information projection
VIPP Variable Information Processing Package
VLF very low frequency
VLSI very large scale integration
VM virtual machine; virtual memory
VMM virtual machine monitor
VM/Prolog Virtual Machine/Programming in Logic
VMS Virtual Memory System
VMT Virtual Memory Technique
VMTSS Virtual Machine Time-sharing System
VNET Virtual Networks
VNL via net loss
VODACOM voice data communication
VODS video operator distress syndrome
vol volume
VOM volt ohmmeter
VOR voice-operated relay

VOS voice operated switch
VOX voice operated control
VPA volume purchase agreement
VPN™ Virtual Private Network (trademark of U.S. Telecom)
VPSS/VF Vector Processing Subsystem/Vector Facility
V+TU voice plus teleprinter unit
VPU video processing unit
VR voltage regulator
VRAM video random access memory
VRC vertical redundancy check
VS variable speed; virtual storage
VSAM Virtual Storage Access Method
VSC variable speed control
VSE virtual storage extended
VSI virtual screen interface
VS1 virtual storage one
VSPC visual storage personal computing
VSS Voltage for Substrate and Sources
VS2 virtual storage two
VT video tape; video terminal
VTAM virtual telecommunications access method; vortex telecommunications access method
VTOC volume table of contents
VTR video tape recorder
VTS/MA virtual terminal session/multiple access
VU voice unit
VW Volkswriter
VWL variable word length

W

w watts; write
WADS Wide Area Data Service
WALT West's Automatic Law Terminal
WAN wide area network
WAP work assignment procedure
WATFIV Waterloo FORTRAN IV (University of Waterloo, Ontario)
WATFOR Waterloo FORTRAN
WATS Wide Area Telecommunications Service
WB wide band
WCS writable control store

wd word
WE write enable
WESTLAW™ West Publishing Company's law research database
WFF well-formed formula
WILS WANG Interactive Learning System
WIN Wollongong Integrated Network
WIP work in progress
WIS Worldwide Information System
WO work order

WOM write optional memory; write only memory
WP word processing
WP/AS word processing/administrative support
WPAAS word processing and administrative support system
WP/DP word processing/data processing system
WPM words per minute

WP/OS word processing/office systems
WPS words per second
wr write
WS-30 WANG system 30
WS working storage; work space
W/S words per second
WSN WANG System Networking
WRU "who are you?" command query
WTO write to operator
WTOR write to operator with reply

X

XA extended architecture
XFER transfer
XMIT transmit
xmt transmit
xmtl transmittal
XNS XEROX Network System
X-OFF transmitter off

X-ON transmitter on
XOR exclusive or
XR external reset
XRF extended reliability feature
xtal crystal
XTC external transmit clock

Y

YACC Yet Another Compiler-Compiler
YES/MVS Yorktown Expert System for Multiple Virtual Storage Environments

YIG yttrium–iron–garnet
yr year
YTD year-to-date
yy year

Z

Z1 Zuse one (a mechanical calculator, after Konrad Zuse)
Z2 Zuse two (electromechanical calculator)
Z3 Zuse three (electromechanical programmed calculator)
Z4 Zuse four (all-purpose relay computer)

Z8 Zilog eight bit one-chip microcomputer (Zilog, Inc.)
Z80 Zilog eight bit microprocessor
Z800 Zilog eight bit microprocessor (Z80 expanded)
Z8000 Zilog sixteen bit microprocessor
ZX80 a microcomputer built by Sinclair Research Ltd., U.K.

2

INFORMATION PROCESSING:
ORGANIZATIONS

(Organizations; Corporations; Associations; Societies; Major Vendors.)

A

AAA American Accounting Association

AAAI American Association for Artificial Intelligence

AAAS American Association for the Advancement of Science

AACE American Association of Cost Engineers

AACSCEDR Associate and Advisory Committee to the Special Committee on Electronic Data Retrieval

ABA American Bankers Association; American Bar Association

ABCS Advanced Business Computer Systems International, Incorporated

ABRACE (Brazilian Association of Electronic Computers)

ACA American Communications Association; Automatic Communications Association

ACBS Accrediting Commission for Business Schools

ACG Atlanta Counseling Group

ACI Apple Computer, Incorporated

ACIS Association for Computing and Information Sciences

ACL Association for Computational Linguistics

ACLS American Council of Learned Societies

ACM Association for Computing Machinery

ACMAC ACM Accreditation Committee

ACME Association of Consulting Management Engineers

ACM-GAMM Association for Computing Machinery/German Association for Applied Mathematics and Mechanics

ACMSC ACM Standards Committee

ACP Applied Computer Products, Incorporated

ACPA Association of Computer Programmers and Anaylsts

ACS Atlanta Computer Society; Australian Computer Society; AVCO Computer Services

ACTS Automatic Computer Telex Services

ACUTE Accountants Computer Users Technical Exchange

ADAPSO Association of Data Processing Service Organizations

ADCU Association of Data Communications Users, Incorporated

ADDS Applied Digital Data Systems Incorporated

ADI American Documentation Institute

ADIS Association for Development of Instructional Systems

ADPCM Association for Data Processing and Computer Management

ADR Applied Data Research

ADS Advanded Digital Systems, Incorporated; Antex Data Systems

AEA American Electronics Association

AECT Association for Educational Communications and Technology

AED Association of Electronics Distributors

AEDP Association of Educational Data Processing

AEDS Association of Electronic Data Systems; Association for Educational Data Systems

AEI Associated Electrical Industries Limited

AEPEM Association of Electronic Parts and Equipment Manufacturers

AFAFC Air Force Accounting and Finance Center

AFCALTIC (French association for computation and data processing)

AFIPS American Federation of Information Processing Societies

AFSCC Air Force Special Communications Center

AFSM Association of Field Service Managers

AFTAC Air Force Technical Application Center

AIA Aerospace Industrial Association

AIB American Institute of Banking

AIC Artificial Intelligence Corporation

AICE American Institute of Consulting Engineers

AICPA American Institute of Certified Public Accountants

AIH Ad Hoc Telephone Users Committee

AIIE American Institute of Industrial Engineers

AIIM Association for Information and Image Management

AIM Association of Information Managers

AIME American Institute of Mechanical Engineers

AISP Association of Information Systems Professionals

ALA American Library Association

ALS Arrix Logic Systems, Incorporated

AMA American Management Association; American Medical Association

AMD Advanced Micro-Devices, Incorporated

AMFIS American Microfilm Information Society

AMI American Microsystems, Incorporated

AMOS American Meteorological Observation Station

AMS American Management Society; Administrative Management Society

ANSI American National Standards Institute

APEX Association of Professional, Executive Clerical and Computer Staff

APICS American Production and Inventory Control Society

ARD Advanced Resource Development

ARMA Association of Records Managers and Administrators; American Records Management Association

ARPA Advanced Research Projects Agency

ASA American Standards Association; American Statistical Association

ASC Alpha Software Corporation; American Satellite Corporation

ASLIB Association of Special Libraries and Information Bureaus

ASM Association for Systems Management

ASME American Society of Mechanical Engineers

ASQC American Society for Quality Control

AST Army Satellite Tracking Center

ASTEC Applied Software Technology

ATG Alcatel-Thomson-Gigadisc

ATI Advanced Technology International, Incorporated

ASTIA Armed Services Technical Information Agency

AT&T American Telephone and Telegraph

B

BAC   Bell Atlantic Corporation

BASF   Badische Anlin Und Soda Fabrik (A German computer products company)

BBC   British Broadcasting Company

BC   Burroughs Corporation

BCAC   British Conference on Automation and Computation

BCDA   Business Computer Dealers Association

BCR   Business Communications Review

BDS   British Computer Society; Business Computer Solutions

BDS   Backus Data Systems, Incorporated

BEA   Business Education Association

BEAMA   British Electrical and Allied Manufacturers

BEC   British Engineers Club

BEMA   Business Equipment Manufacturers Association

B&H   Bell and Howell Company

BIEE   British Institute of Electrical Engineers

BIMCAM   British Industrial Measuring and Control Apparatus Manufacturer's Association

BIO   Biological Information Processing Organization

BISC   Business Information Systems Company

BL   Bell Labs (Bell Telephone laboratories)

BLS   Bureau of Labor Statistics

BOC   Bell Operating Company

BSI   British Standards Institution

BTAP   Bond Trade Analysis Program

BTS   Business Telecommunication Services

BUNCH   Burroughs, Univac (Sperry), NCR, CDC, and Honeywell (the five large-scale computer manufacturers, not including IBM)

C

CAI   Computer Application, Incorporated; Computer Associates International, Incorporated

CAID   Canadian Association for Information Science

CALCOMP   California Computer Products, Incorporated

CAMI   Computer Aided Manufacturing International

CAN/OLE   Canadian On-line Enquiry (of CISTI)

CAN/SDI   Canadian Selective Dissemination of Information (of CISTI)

CANSIM   Canadian Socio-Economic Information Management System

CAP   Council on Advanced Programming

CASLIS   Canadian Association of Special Libraries and Information Services

CBC   Canadian Broadcasting Corporation

CBEMA   Canadian Business Equipment Manufacturers Association; Computer and Business Equipment Manufacturers Association

CBS   Columbia Broadcasting Company

CCA   Cambridge Computer Associates, Incorporated; Computer Corporation of America

CCC   Computer Control Company; Computech Consulting Canada, Limited

CCI   Computer Consoles, Incorporated

CCITT   Consultative Committee on International Telephone and Telegraph

CCL   Cybernetion Consultants, Limited (Canada)

CCS   Computer Consulting Service;

Contel Cado Systems Corporation; Corporate Contingency Services

CCT Custom Computer Technology

CDC Canada Development Corporation; Control Data Corporation

CDI Control Data Institute

CDPS Computing and Data Processing Society (Canada)

CDRS Comdisco Disaster Recovery Services

CDS Concord Data Systems

CEC Capital Equipment Corporation

CECUA Conference on European Computer Users Associations

CEIR Corporation for Economic Industrial Research

CEPS Corporate Electronics Publishing Show

CESR Canadian Electronic Sales Representatives

CGC Compugraphic Corporation

CGS Cambridge Graphic Systems

CIA Central Intelligence Agency

CII Communication Industries, Incorporated; Computers International, Incorporated; Cottage Industries, Incorporated

CIPM Council for International Progress in Management

CIPS Canadian Information Processing Society

CIR Center for International Research

CIS Contel Information Systems Incorporated

CISD Computer and Information Systems Department

CISTI Canadian Institute for Scientific and Technical Information

CITE Council of Institute of Telecommunications Engineers

CITEL Inter-American Telecommunications Commission

CLC Computer Learning Center

CLR Counsel on Library Resources

CMA Canadian Manufacturers Association

CMC California Micro Computer; Canadian Marconi Corporation

CNI Consolidated Networks, Incorporated

CODASYL Conference on Data Systems Languages

CODE Coordinators of Data Processing Education

COLRAD College on Research and Development

COMSAT Communications Satellite Corporation

COMTECH Computer Technical Services, Incorporated

COSHTI Council for Science and Technological Information

COSOS Conference on Self-Operating Systems

COT Coalition for Office Technology

COTC Canadian Overseas Telecommunications Corporation

CPI Computer Processes, Incorporated

CPM Computer Parts Merchants, Incorporated

CPRG Computer Personnel Research Group

CSA Canadian Standards Association; Computer Science Association. (Canada); Contract Services Associates

CSC Computer Sciences Canada Limited

CSI Communications Solutions, Incorporated; Creative Strategies International

CSIRO Commonwealth Scientific and Industrial Research Organization

CSSI Computer Software and Services Industry

CTCA Canadian Telecommunications Carriers Association

CTG Computer Task Group

CTI Computer Technology Innovations

CTS Computer Training Services, Incorporated

CTUNA Commercial Telegraphers Union

CWA Communication Workers of America

CWO Corvallis Workstation Operation

D

DARPA Defense Advanced Research Projects Agency

DATDC Data Analysis and Technique Development Center

DATEL II RCA Global Communication Data Service in Conjunction with TELENET

DCA Digital Computers Association; Digital Communications Associates

DCMA Defense Contract Management Association

DCUG Datamac Computer Users Group

DDC Defense Documentation Center for Scientific and Technical Information

DDI Database Designing Incorporated

DEC Digital Equipment Corporation

DECUS Digital Equipment Computer Users Society

DEMA Data Entry Management Association

DESC Defense Electronics Supply Center

DEUA Digitronics Equipment Users Association

DGC Data General Corporation

DPMA Data Processing Management Association

DRC Dataram Corporation; Decca Radar Canada Limited

DRI Digital Research Incorporated

DSG Design Systems Group

DSI Data Systems International, Incorporated

DSMG Designated Systems Management Group

DSS Distributed Software Systems

DTC Display Telecommunications Corporation

DUO Datatron Users Organization

E

EA Electronic Arts

EAI Electronics Associates, Incorporated

EATCS European Association of Theoretical Computer Science

ECD Energy Conversion Devices, Incorporated

ECI Eeco Computer, Incorporated

ECMA European Computer Manufacturer's Association

ECPI Electronic Computer Programming Institute

ECS Eastern Computer Services, Incorporated (Canada)

EDI Electronic Data Interchange

EDPI Electronic Data Processing Industries Limited (Canada); Electronic Data Processing Institute

EDRI Electronic Distributors' Research Institute

EDS Electronic Data Systems Corporation

EEA Electronic Engineering Association

EEOC Equal Employment Opportunity Commission

EFOC/LAN European Fiberoptics Communications and Local Area Network Exposition

EIA Electronic Industries Association

EIAJ Electronic Industries Association of Japan

EIES Electronic Information Exchange System

EIS Economic Information Systems, Incorporated

EIT Electronic Information Technology

EJCC Eastern Joint Computer Conference

EMG   Eastern Management Group
EMR   Electromechanical Research, Incorporated
EMS   Educational Microcomputer Technology
ENC   European Networking Center
EPIE   Educational Products Information Exchange

EPMA   Electronic Parts Manufacturers Association
ERA   Engineering Research Associates
ERG   Emprical Research Group, Incorporated
ESI   Executive Systems, Incorporated
ESMA   Electronic Sales and Marketing Association

F

FACT   Foundation for Advanced Computer Technology
FBI   Federal Bureau of Investigation
FCC   Federal Communications Commission
FDP   Future Data Processors (DMPA)

FEDC   Federal Equipment Data Center
FEI   Financial Executives Institute
FMA   Forsythe/McArthur Associates, Incorporated
FOAC   Federal Office Automation Conference

G

GATTIS   Georgia Institute of Technology and Technical Information Science
GC   General Communications Incorporated
GCE   Government Computer Expo
GCI   Graphic Communications Incorporated
GDC   General Datacomm, Incorporated
GE   General Electric Company

GEISCO   General Electric Information Services Company
GET   General Electric Computer Users Group
GI   General Instruments Corporation
GPO   Government Printing Office
GSA   General Services Administration
GTE   General Telephone and Electronics

H

H   Honeywell Information Systems, Incorporated
HCUA   Honeywell Computer Users Association
HDS   Human Designed Systems, Incorporated
HIS   Honeywell Information Systems, Incorporated

HIIS   Honeywell Institute for Information Science
HMSS   Hospital Management Systems Society
HP   Hewlett-Packard Company
HRSP   Association of Human Resource System Professionals

I

IACP International Association of Computer Programmers

IACSM International Association of Computer Service Managers

IAM/TMD Institute of Administrative Management/Telecommunications Managers Division

IAS Immedicat Access Store

IASA Insurance Accounting and Statistical Association

IAT Institute for Advanced Technology

IBFI International Business Forms Industries

IBM International Business Machines Corporation

IBS Institute for Basic Standards; International Business Services

ICA Industrial Communications Association; International Computer Association

ICC IBM Credit Corporation; International Computer Center

ICCA Independent Computer Consultants Association

ICCP Institute for Certification of Computer Professionals

ICEM International Council for Educational Media

ICIP International Conference on Information Processing

ICL International Computers Limited

ICS Institute for Computer Sciences; International Computer Systems

ICT Institute for Computer Technology

IDC International Data Corporation

IDCMA Independent Data Communications Manufacturing Association

IDS Integrated Data Systems, Incorporated

IECES Institute of Electronic Communications Engineers of Japan

IEEE Institute of Electrical and Electronics Engineers

IEL International Electrochemical Commission

IFCS International Federation of Computer Sciences

IFD International Federation for Documentation

IFIP International Federation for Information Processing

IFIPS International Federation of Information Processing Societies

IIA Information Industry Association

IIN IBM Information Network

IIS IBM Information Services; Institute of Information Scientists

IJCAI International Joint Conference on Artificial Intelligence

IMI International Marketing Institute

IMIS Integrated Management Information System

IMS Industrial Management Society; Institute of Management Sciences; International Management Services, Incorporated

INFONET Network of Computer Sciences Corporation

INTELSAT International Satellite Service

IPA Information Processing Association

IS Interactive Structures, Incorporated

ISA Information Science Associates; Instrument Society of America; International Systems Associates Limited

IS&CG Information Systems and Communications Group

ISL Inbucon Services Limited (Canada)

ISM International Software Marketing, Incorporated

ISO Independent Sales Organization (WANG); International Standards Organization

ISSCO Integrated Software Systems Corporation

ITC International Technology Corporation

ITD Information Technologies Division (of MMDS)

ITE Institute of Telecommunication Engineers

ITT International Telephone and Telegraph Company

ITU International Telecommunication Union

IWP International Word Processing Association

J

JAS Johnson Associates Software
JCUDI Japan Computer Usage Development Institute
JE Jensen Engineering, Incorporated

JEEC Japanese Electronic Computer Company
JIAC Joint Automatic Control Conference

K

KAEDS Keystone Association for Educational Data Systems

KCI Keyboard Communications, Incorporated

L

LDC Lotus Development Corporation
LDP Lomas Data Products, Incorporated
LMC Logical Micro-Computer Company

LMI Laboratory Microsystems Incorporated
LSA Logistic Systems Architects
LSI Lear Siegler, Incorporated

M

MAI Management Assistance Incorporated
MBI Microcomputer Business International
MCA Massachusetts Computer Associates, Incorporated
MCBA Minicomputer Business Applications
MCBS Microcomputer Business Services
MCC Microelectronics and Computer

Technology Corporation
MCCA Mobil Communications Corporation of America
MCUG Military Computer Users Group
MDC Mead Data Central
MECCA Minnesota Educational Computing Corporation
MES Maple Equipment Specialists
MIC Management Information Corporation

MIT Massachusetts Institute of Technology

MMA Microcomputer Managers Association

MMDS Martin Marietta Data Systems

MOOTECH Modern Technologies International

MPI Magnetic Peripherals, Incorporated

MPSG Marketing Programs and Services Group

MRI Management Recruiters International

MSA Management Science of America

MSC Management Systems Corporation

MST Media Systems Technology, Incorporated

MTC Microelectronics Technology Corporation

MTI Memory Technologies, Incorporated

N

NAA National Association of Accountants

NABAC National Association for Bank Audit, Control and Operation

NACAA National Association of Computer Assisted Analysts

NACC National Automatic Controls Conference

NAED National Association of Electrical Distributors

NAEDS National Association of Educational Data Systems

NAI Network Applications, Incorporated

NAPM National Association of Purchasing Management

NARUC National Association of Regulatory Utility Commissioners

NAS National Advanced Systems

NASA National Aeronautics and Space Administration

NASIS National Association for State Information Systems

NASPA National Association for Public Accountants

NATA North American Telecommunications Association

NATTS National Association of Trade and Technical Schools

NAVA National Audio Visual Association

NBS National Bureau of Standards

NCC National Computer Conference; National Computing Center

NCI National Computer Institute; Northeast Computer Institute

NCN National Computer Network

NCR National Cash Register Company

NCS National Communications Systems

NDD National Distribution Division (of IBM)

NEA National Education Association

NEC Nippon Electronics Corporation

NECA National Exchange Carriers Association

NECS Nationwide Eduational Computer Service

NEDA National Electronics Distributors Association

NEEDS New England Educational Data Systems

NEFO National Electronics Facilities Organization

NEMA National Electrical Manufacturers Association

NFTW National Federation of Telephone Workers

NIOSH National Institute of Occupational Safety and Health

NIRI National Information Research Institute

NISC National Information Systems Corporation

NJCC National Joint Computers Committee

NMA National Management Association; National Microfilm Association

NOAC National Operations and Automation Conference

NOMA National Office Management Association

NOMDA National Office Machine Dealers Association

NOPA National Office Products Association

NRC National Research Council

NSA National Security Agency

NSC National Semiconductor Corporation

NTI Northern Telecom, Incorporated

NTIS National Technical Information Service

NTT Nippon Telegraph and Telephone Company

NWB North Western Bell

O

OABETA Office Appliance and Business Equipment Trades Association

OASIS Office Administration Services and Integrated Systems, Incorporated

OCLI Optical Coating Laboratories, Incorporated

OEA Office Executives Association

OEMI Original Equipment Manufacturers Institute

OMAT Office of Manpower and Automatic Training

ORSA Operations Research Society of America

OSEC Office Systems Education and Counseling

OSI Optical Storage International

OSIS Office of Scientific Information Service

OSOG Office Systems Owners Group

OTMA Office Technology Management Association

OTRG Office Technology Research Group

P

PC Philco Corporation

PCI Prime Computer, Incorporated

PDC Percom Data Corporation

PGCS Professional Group Communication Systems

PGEC Professional Group Electronic Computers

PII Performance Interconnect, Incorporated

PPA Professional Programmers Association

PTT Postal, Telegraph and Telephone Administration

PUC Public Utilities Commission

Q

QCS Quality Computer Services, Incorporated

QTC Quantitative Technology Corporation

R

RCA Radio Corporation of America

RDS Relational Database Systems

REI Recognition Equipment, Incorporated; Research Equipment, Incorporated

REMRAND Remington Rand Univac (now Univac Division of Sperry Rand Corporation)

RM Rand McFarland Company

RRU Remington Rand Univac (now Univac Division of Sperry Rand Corporation)

RTC Realtime Corporation Limited (Canada)

RTI Relational Technology, Incorporated

S

SABE Society for Automation in Business Education

SAM Society for the Advancement of Management

SAS System Automation Software Company

SBC Service Bureau Corporation

SCAMC Symposium on Computer Applications in Medical Care

SCD System Communications Division (of IBM)

SCM Smith Corona Merchang Company

SDC Systems Development Corporation

SDD System Development Division (of IBM)

SDI Software Digest Incorporated

SDS Scientific Data Systems Incorporated

SEAS Share European Association

SEDS Society for Educational Data Systems

SEL Systems Engineering Lab

SEM Security Engineered Machinery

SI Systems Industries, Incorporated

SIGACT A special interest group on automata and computability theory of of ACM

SIGADA A special interest group on ADA of ACM

SIGALP A special interst group on a programming language of ACM

SIGARCH A special interest group on computer architecture of ACM

SIGART A special interest group on artificial intelligence of ACM

SIGBDP A special interest group on business data processing of ACM

SIGBIO A special interest group on biomedical computing of ACM

SIGCAPH A special interest group on computers and the physically handicapped of ACM

SIGCAS A special interest group on computers and society of ACM

SIGCHI A special interest group on computer and human interaction of ACM

SIGCOMM A special interest group on data communications of ACM

SIGCOSIM A special interest group on computer systems installation management of ACM

SIGCPR A special interest group on computer personnel research of ACM

SIGCSE A special interest group on computer science education of ACM

SIGCUE A special interest group on computer users in education of ACM

SIGDA A special interest group on design automation of ACM

SIGDOC A special interest group on documentation of ACM

SIGFIDET A special interest group on file description and translation of ACM

SIGGRAPH A special interest group for graphical display of ACM

SIGIR A special interest group on information retrieval of ACM

SIG/LA A special interest group library automation and networks of ACM

SIGMA A special interest group on science in general management of ACM

SIGMAP A special interest group on mathematical programming of ACM

SIGME A special interest group on measurement and evaluation of ACM

SIGMICRO A special interest group on microprogramming of ACM

SIGMOD A special interest group on management of data of ACM

SIGNUM A special interest group on numerical mathematics of ACM

SIGOA A special interest group on office automation of ACM

SIGOPS A special interest group on operating systems of ACM

SIGPLAN A special interest group on programming languages of ACM

SIGREAL A special interest group on real time processing of ACM

SIGSAC A special interest group on security, audit and control of ACM

SIGSAM A special interest group on symbolic and algebraic manipulation of ACM

SIGSIM A special interest group on simulation of ACM

SIGSMALL/PC A special interest group on small and personal computing systems and applications of ACM

SIGSOFT A special interest group on software engineering of ACM

SIGUCCS A special interest group on university and college computing services of ACM

SIG/UOI A special interest group on user on-line interaction of ACM

SIM Society for Information Management

SLA Special Libraries Association

SMA Systems Management Associates; Systems Management Association

SMC Science Management Corporation

SME Society of Manufacturing Engineers

SMIS Society for Management Information Systems

SMS Specialized Management Service, Incorporated

SNET Southern New England Telephone

SPCC Sanyo PC Computer Club

SPDP Society of Professional Data Processors

SPMC Society of Professional Management Consultants

SRL Sinclare Research Limited (U.K.)

SSI Satellite Software International

SSL Symbionics Systems Limited (Canada)

STC Society for Technical Communication; Software Technology for Computers; Storage Technology Corporation

STI Signal Technology, Incorporated

SWIFT Society for Worldwide Interbank Financial Telecommunications

T

TCC Telemetry Standards Coordination Committee

TCTS Trans Canada Telephone System (Canada)

TCWG Telecommunications Working Group

TI Texas Instruments

TIC Technology International Corporation

TIFI The Integrated Facilities Institute

TPI Telecom Plus International

TRI-CON Tri-Continental Leasing Corporation

TRS Tandy-Radio Shack (Tandy Corporation)

TSD Telecommunications and Systems Division (Philips International)
TSI Typography Systems International

TTI Tempest Technologies, Incorporated

U

UAIDE Users of Automatic Information Display Equipment
UCC United Computing Corporation; University Computing Company
UCL Univac Canada Limited
UDCI United Data Centers, Incorporated
UDPC Univac Data Processing Center
UDS Universal Data Systems
UL Underwriters Laboratories, Incorporated
USAAVA United States Army Audio-Visual Agency
USACC United States Army Communication Command

USACEEIA United States Army Communications-Electronics Engineering Installation Agency
USACSSEC United States Army Computer Systems Support and Evaluation Command
USASI United States of America Standards Institute (now ANSI)
USCI United States Computers, Incorporated
UTCC United Technologies Company
UTP United Technical Products, Incorporated
UUA Univac Users Association

V

VDA Viewdata Corporation of America
VDC Venture Development Corporation
VICOM International Association of Visual Communications Management

VIDPI Visually Impaired Data Processors International
VPI Viatron Programming, Incorporated

W

WCC Wingate Computer Center
WCCE World Conference on Computers in Education
WCS Welby Computer Services Limited (Canada)
WDC Westlake Data Corporation
WDPL Western Data Processing Center (University of California)

WEMA Western Electronics Manufacturers Association
WISC Wang Information Services Corporation
WISE World Information Systems Exchange
WUI Western Union International

3

BUSINESS AND THE LAW

(Office Administration; Accounting; Finance; Stock Exchanges; Legal Terms; Law Reports; Business Associations; Government; Time Zones)

A

AAA American Arbitration Association; approved as amended

AACSL American Association for the Comparative Study of Law

A&M agricultural and mechanical

ABA American Bankers Association; American Bar Association

ab init ab initio (L., from the beginning)

abr abridged

abt about

ABTA American Board of Trial Advocates

acc account

acc accepted; account; accountant

ack acknowledge

acct account

A/cs Pay accounts payable

A/cs Rec accounts receivable

ACRL Association of College and Reference Libraries

ACTL American College of Trial Lawyers

AD anno domini (L., in the year of our Lord); Appellate Division (Supreme Court) New York

ad administration

ADA assistant district attorney

add addendum; addition

addn addition

addnl additional

ad fin ad finem (L., at or to the end)

ad int ad interim (L., for the intervening time)

ad loc ad locum (L., at or to the place)

Adm admiral

admin administration

admix administratrix

admrx administratrix

admx administratrix

ADS autograph document signed

ads ad sectam (L., at the suit of)

ADT Atlantic Daylight Time

adv adversus; advocate

ad val ad valorem (L., according to value)

aet aetatis (L., of age)

aetat aetatis (L., of age)

aff affairs

affd affirmed; affirmed by memorandum opinion

affi affidavit

afft affidavit

AFLA American Foreign Law Association

AG attorney general

AGO adjutant general's office

agric agriculture

agt agreement

AI ad interim (L., for the intervening time)

AID Agency for International Development (United States)
AIM American Institute of Management
AINL Association of Immigration and Nationality Lawyers
AJ associate justice
aka also known as
ald alderman
ALI American Law Institute
ALJ administrative law judge
ALR American Law Reports
ALS autograph letter signed
ALSA American Law Student Association
am ante meridiem (L., before noon)
amb ambassador
Am Dec American Decisions
amdt amendment
AMEX American Stock Exchange
Am Jur American Jurisprudence
amt amount
ann annals
annot annotated; annotation
anon anonymous
ANS autograph note signed
ans answer
a/o (on) account of
AOC administrative office of the courts
AP accounts payable; additional premium
ap apud (L., according to)

a/p accounts payable
APO army post office
app apparent; apparently; appeal; appellate; appendix; appointed
app dism appeal dismissed
app pend appeal pending
approx approximately
apt apartment
ar arrival
a/r accounts receivable
art article
AS administrative support
ASE Alberta Stock Exchange
ASAP as soon as possible
asap as soon as possible
ass association
assn association
assoc associate; association
asst assistant
AST Atlantic Standard Time
at attorney
ATL anti trust law
ATLA American Trial Lawyers Association
att attorney
atty attorney
aud audit; auditor
auth author; authority
AV ad valorum (L., according to value); audiovisual
avg average
AVP Administrative Vice President

B

b bachelor; bar
BA business administration
BAJI basic approved jury instructions
bal balance
bankr bankruptcy
Barb Barbour's Supreme Court Reports, New York
Barn&Ald Barnewall and Alderson's King's Bench Reports (U.K.)
barr barrister
BB bail bond; bank book
BBB Better Business Bureau
BC bail court; before Christ

BCL bachelor of canon law; bachelor of civil law; bachelor of commercial law
BCS bachelor of commercial science
BD back dividend; bank draft; bills discounted; brought down
bd bond
BE bill of exchange
BF brought forward
BFS basic financial statements
BG bonded goods
bio biography
Bisph Eg Bispham's Equity
bk bank; book

bkcy bankruptcy
BL bachelor of law
bl bill of lading
B/L bill of lading
Bl Comm Blackstone's Commentaries
bldg building
BLL bachelor of laws
BN bank note
BO branch office; broker's order; buyer's option
BP bills payable
BPB bank post bill
BR bank rate; bills receivable

BS balance sheet; bill of sale
BS BA bachelor of science in business administration
BSE Boston Stock Exchange
BSL bachelor of science in law
BST Bering Standard Time
BT board of trade
BTA board of tax appeals
BTU British thermal unit
bull bulletin
BUS business
Bus&Prof business & professions
BV book value

C

c cents; century; chancellor
CA chartered accountant; chief accountant; court of appeal
C/A capital account; credit account; current account
CAA Canadian Author's Association
CAAA Canadian Association of Advertising Agencies
CACUL Canadian Association of College and University Libraries
CAF clerical, administrative, and fiscal; cost and freight; cost, assurance and freight
calc calculating
CALL Canadian Association of Law Libraries
Cal Rptr California Reporter
CAMC Canadian Association of Management Consultants
canc cancelled
C&F cost and freight
cap capital; capitalize
CAPA Canadian Association of Purchasing Agents
CAPL Canadian Association of Public Libraries
caps capitals
CARD Canadian Advertising Rates and Data
carr carriers
cas casualty
CASE Counselling Assistance to Small Enterprise (Canada)

CASLIS Canadian Association of Special Libraries and Information Sciences
cat catalog
CATA Canadian Air Transportation Administration
CAV curia advisari vult (L., the court will be advised)
CB cashbook; common bench
CBA Canadian Bar Association; Canadian Booksellers Association
CB Chicago Board of Trade
CBD cash before delivery
CBO Chicago Board Options Exchange
CBPC Canadian Book Publishers Council
CC chief clerk; chief counsel; circuit court; city council; civil cases; civil code; county court; criminal cases; crown cases
cc carbon copy; chapters
CCA circuit court of appeals
CCAB Canadian Circulation Audit Board
CCAF Canadian Comprehensive Auditing Foundation
CCH Commerce Clearing House
CCLS court of claims
CCLSR court of claims reports
CCMA Canadian Council of Management Associations
CCP Code of Civil Procedure; court of common pleas

CCPA court of customs and patent appeals

CD certificate of deposit; congressional district

CDT Central Daylight Time

CE caveat emptor

CEO chief executive officer

cert certiorari

cert den certiorari denied

CESO Canadian Executive Services Overseas

CF carried forward; cost and freight

cf confer (L., compare)

CFI cost, freight and insurance

CFS consolidated financial statements

CFTC Commodity Futures Trading Commission

CGSB Canadian Government Specifications Board

ch chairman; chapter

chg charge

chm chairman

chs chapters

CH clearinghouse; court house

chron chronology

CI cost and insurance

CICA Canadian Institute of Chartered Accountants

CIDA Canadian International Development Agency

CIF cost, insurance and freight

cir circuit

cit citation

civ civil

civ proc civil procedure

CJ chief justice, chief judge

CJS Corpus Juris Secundum

ck check

CL civil law; civil liberties; common law

cl clerk

CLA Canadian Library Association

CLB bachelor of civil law

CLD doctor of civil law

CLI cost of living index

CM causa mortis (L., by reason of death); court martial

CMA cash management accounts; court of military appeals

CMHC Canadian Mortgage and Housing Corporation

CMR court of military review

CMTP Canadian Manpower Training Program

CN credit note

CO cash order

Co company

c/o care of; carry over

COD cash on delivery; collect on delivery

COL cost of living

com commercial

COMDA Canadian Office Machine Dealers Association

comr commissioner

comm commission

comp compensation; compounded

compt comptroller

conc concurring

conf conference

Cong Congress; Congressional

const constitution

contd continued

co-op co-operative

cor correspondent; correspondence

corp corporation

corr correspondence

COS cash on shipment

CP court of probate

CPA certified public accountant

CPD common pleas division

CPFF cost plus fixed fee

CPI Consumer Price Index

CPIC Canadian Police Information Center

CPLR Civil Practice Law and Rules

CPPA Canadian Periodical Publishers Association

CQS consolidated quotation system

CR credit

cr credit; creditor

crim criminal

CRTC Canadian Radio and Television Commission

CS capital stock; civil service

cs capital stock; civil service

CSA Canadian Standards Association

CSE Cincinnati Stock Exchange

CST Central Standard Time

ct court; county

CTA cum testamento annexo (L., with the will annexed)

CTCLS court of claims

ctr center
cur currency
CWO cash with order

cwo cash with order
cwt hundredweight
Cyc Cyclopedia of Law and Procedure

D

D date
DA deposit account; district attorney
DAD deputy assistant director
DAT differential aptitude test
db daybook; debenture
DBA Dealer Bank Association
d/b/a doing business as
dbn de bonis non (L., of the goods not)
DC defense counsel; district court; doctor of chiropractic
DCF discounted cash flow; document coding form
DCL doctor of canon law; doctor of civil law; doctor of commercial law
DCnl doctor of canon law
D Comp L doctor of comparative law
DCS deputy clerk of sessions
DD demand draft
dd delivered
D/D demand draft
d/d delivered
deb debenture
deben debenture
def defendant; defense
deg degree
Del Ch Delaware Chancery Reports
den denied
depo deposition
depr depreciation
dept department; deponent; deputy
DF damage free
DG Dei gratia (L., by the grace of God);

director general
dis dissenting
disc discount
div dividend; division
DJ district judge
DJIA Dow Jones Industrial Average
DJS doctor of judicial science
DL demand loan; doctor of law
DLO dead letter office
dls/shr dollars per share
DO district officer
doc document
dol dollar
doz dozen
DP data processing
DPB deposit passbook
dpt department
DQ direct question
DR debit; deposit receipt
dr debit
Dr Jur doctor juris (L., doctor of law)
Dr LL doctor of laws
DS deputy sheriff
dps decessit sine prole (L., died without issue)
DST daylight saving time
dup duplicate
DV Deo volente (L. God willing)
DWI died without issue
D/y delivery
dz dozen

E

ea each
EC exempli causa (L., for example)
EDT Eastern Daylight Time

eff effective
eg exempli gratia (L., for example)
encl enclosure

EOM   end of month
eom   end of month
EP   excess profits
EPT   excess profits tax
ER   en route
ES   executive secretary
ESOP   employee stock ownership plan
EST   Eastern Standard Time
ETA   estimated time of arrival
et al   et alia (L., and others)
et seq   et sequens (L., and the following)
et seq   et sequentes or et sequentia (L., and those that follow)

et ux   et uxor (L., and wife)
ex   executive; exhibit
exec   executive
Exec Order   Executive Order
Exhib   exhibit
exp   expense
exr   executor
ex rel   ex relatione (L., by or on the relation or information of)
exrx   executrix
ext   extention; external; extreme
exx   executrix

F

FA   felonius assault; financial advisor
FAA   free of all average
FAD   free air delivered
FAQ   fair average quality
FAS   free alongside ship
FB   freight bill
FBA   Federal Bar Association
FBM   foot board measure
fcap   foolscap
FCC   Federal Communications Commission; First Class Commission
FC&S   free of capture and seizure
FD   free delivery
FDIC   Federal Deposit Insurance Corporation
fec   fecit (L., he made it)
Fed   federal
fed   federal
Fed Cas   Federal Cases
Fed R Civ Proc   Federal Rules of Civil Procedure
Fed R Crim Proc   Federal Rules of Criminal Procedure
ff   fecerunt (L., they made)
FFT   for further transfer
FIB   free into barge
FICA   Federal Insurance Contributions Act

fid   fiduciary
fi fa   fieri facias
fin   financial
fisc   fiscal
FIT   Federal Income Tax
fn   footnote
fndn   foundation
fns   footnotes
FOB   free on board
FOC   free of charge
FOQ   free on quay
FOR   free on rail
FOS   free on steamer
FOT   free on truck
FP   financial planning; fully paid
FPO   fleet post office (postal service)
FRD   Federal Rules Decisions
FRS   Federal Reserve System
FSLIC   Federal Savings and Loan Insurance Corporation
FTC   Federal Trade Commission
F Supp   Federal Supplement
FY   fiscal year
FYA   for your approval
FYE   fiscal year ending
FYI   for your information

G

GA   general average
GAO   General Accounting Office
GAT   Greenwich apparent time
GAW   guaranteed annual wage
GC   general counsel
GCA   general claim agent
GCT   Greenwich civil time
GFA   general freight agent
GJ   grand jury
GJ   graduate in law
GM   general manager

GMT   Greenwich mean time
GNP   gross national product
GO   general office
GOP   Grand Old Party
GPA   general passenger agent
GPO   government printing office
gr   gross
GRI   guaranteed retirement income
GS   general secretary
GST   Greenwich siderial time

H

HB   house bill
HC   House of Commons
HCL   high cost of living
hdqrs   headquarters
HEW   Health, Education & Welfare (U.S. government department)
hg   hearing
hg den   hearing denied
Hon   honorable

HP   hire purchase; House of Parliament
HR   home rule; House of Representatives
HRD   human resources department
HQ   headquarters
hrs   hours
HUD   Housing and Urban Development (U.S. government department)

I

IA   incorporated accountant
IALS   International Association of Legal Science
I&E   information and education
I&P   indexed and paged
I&R   initiative and referendum
I&S   inspection and security; inspection and survey
IB   Investment Dealers Association of Canada; invoice book
IBA   Independent Bar Association; International Bar Association
IBI   invoice book inwards
ibid   ibidem (L., in the same place)

IC   in charge; information center
ICJ   International Commission of Jurists; International Court of Justice
ID   identification
id   idem (L., the same); identification
IF   ipe fecit (L., he did it himself)
IFB   invitation for bid
IG   inspector general
II   inventory and inspection
ILA   International Law Association
ILAA   International Legal Aid Association
Inc   incorporated
inc   inclosed

ins   insurance
int   interest
inv   invoice
invt   inventory
IOU   I owe you
IP   installment paid
IQ   intelligence quotient
iq   idem quod (L., the same as)

IRA   Individual Retirement Account
IRO   Inland Revenue Officer
IRC   Internal Revenue Code
IRS   Internal Revenue Service
ISC   interstate commerce
ISE   Intermountain Stock Exchange
ITC   investment tax credit
IV   increased value

J

J   journal; judge; Justice
JA   joint account; judge advocate
JAG   judge advocate general
JB   jurum baccalaureus (L., bachelor of laws)
JC   jurisconsultus (L., jurisconsultant); justice clerk; juvenile court
J Can B   Juris canna doctor (L., bachelor of canon law)
J Can D   juris canna doctor (L., doctor of canon law)
JCB   juris canonici baccalaureus (L., bachelor of canon law); juris civilis baccalaureus (L., bachelor of civil law)
JCD   juris canonici doctor (L., doctor of canon law); juris civilis doctor (L., doctor of civil law)

JCL   juris canonici licentiatus (L., licentiate in canon law)
JCM   juris civilis magister (L., master of civil law)
JD   juris doctor (L., doctor of law); jurum doctor (L., doctor of laws); jury duty; Justice Department; juvenile delinquent
JJ   judges
JM   juris master (L., master of laws)
JNOV   judgment not withstanding verdict
JP   justice of the peace
JSC   joint stock company
JSD   jurum scientiae doctor (L., doctor of the science of the law)
jurisp   jurisprudence
jus   justice

L

L   lawyer
LA   law agent; legislative assembly
law   lawyer
LB   local board
LC   law court; letters and cards (postal service); letter of credit; Library of Congress
LCJ   lord chief justice
LCM   legis comparativae magister (L., master of comparative law)
LE   labor exchange
led   ledger

leg   legal; legislative
legis   legislation
LJ   lord justice
LL   limited liability
LLB   legum baccalaureus (L., bachelor of laws)
LLD   legum doctor (L., doctor of laws)
LS   listed securities
LSAT   legal scholastic aptitude test
LT   legal tender
ltd   limited

M

MALD   master of arts in law and diplomacy
max   maximum
MBA   master of business administration
MC   member of congress
MCJ   master of comparative jurisprudence
MCL   master of civil law; master of comparative law
M Comp L   master of comparative law
MDT   Mountain Daylight Time
Messrs   Misters
mfg   manufacturing
mgmt   management
mgr   manager
min   minimum
misc   miscellaneous
MJ   military judge
ML   magister legum (L., master of laws)
M Laws   master of laws

MLT   master of law and taxation
MO   mail order; money order
mo   month
mod   modified
MP   member of parliament
MPL   master of patent law
MR   master of the rolls
MR=MC   marginal revenue = marginal cost
MRP   materials requirement planning
MSCJ   master of science in criminal justice
MSE   Montreal Stock Exchange
MSRB   Municipal Securities Rulemaking Board
MST   Mountain Standard Time
MTM   methods time measurement
MV   market value
MWSE   Midwest Stock Exchange, Incorporated

N

n   footnote
NASD   National Association of Securities Dealers
natl   national
NB   nota bene (L., note well)
NBS   National Bureau of Standards
n/c   no charge
NCCL   National Council of Canadian Labour
NEI   not elsewhere included
NEM   not elsewhere mentioned
nem con   nemine contradicente (L., no one contradicting)
nem dis   nemine dissentiente (L., no one dissenting)
NES   not elsewhere specified
NF   no funds
NG   no good
ni pri   nisi prius (L., unless before)
nl   non licet (L., Latin is not permitted); non liquet (L., it is not clear)

NLRB   National Labor Relations Board
No   number
nol pros   nolle prosequi (L., to be unwilling to prosecute)
non obst   non obstante (L., notwithstanding)
non pros   non prosequitur (L., he does not prosecute)
non seq   non sequitur
NOS   not otherwise specified
Nos   numbers
note   footnote
nov   non obstante veredicto (L., notwithstanding the verdict)
NP   notary public
NPL   non personal liability
NPV   no par value
NR   net register; no risk
NS   not specified
NSA   National Secretaries Association
NSF   not sufficient funds

NSCC National Securities Clearing Corporation

NYFE New York Futures Exchange
NYSE New York Stock Exchange

O

OA office automation; other articles (postal service)
o/a on account; open account
OBL order bill of lading
OC office copy; over charge
oc ope consilio (L., by paid and counsel); opere citato (L., in the work cited)
OD overdraft; overdrawn
ofc office
OL occupational level; overload
OMB Office of Management and Budget
op cit opere citato (L., in the work cited)

opn opinion
OPEC Organization of Petroleum-Exporting Countries
OPP out of print at present
org organization
orig original
OS out of stock
OSC Ontario Securities Commission; order to show cause
OSHA Occupational Safety and Health Administration
OT overtime
OTC over the counter (stock trading)
oz ounce

P

p page
pa per annum
PABX private automated branch exchange
P&I protection and indemnity
para paragraph
Pat Pend patent pending
PBA permanent budget account
PC parliamentary case; privy council
PCB petty cash book
PCS principle clerk of session
PCSE Pacific Stock Exchange, Incorporated
PD per diem (L., by the day); post dated
pd paid
PDT Pacific Daylight Time
PE probable error
PEG prior endorsement guaranteed
per proc per procuration (L., by the agency of)
petn petition
PHV pro hace vice (L., for this occasion)

PI preliminary injunction; private investigator; profitability index
P&L profit and loss
PLS professional legal secretary
PLSC project level steering committee
PM pay master
PMH production per man-hour
PN promissory note
PO postal order; post office; purchase order
POD pay on delivery
POS point of sale
PP parcel post; postage paid; prepaid
pp pages
PPA per power of attorney
pres president
PR public relations
PS post script
PSA Public Security Association
PSC personal steering committee
PSE Philadelphia Stock Exchange, Incorporated

PST Pacific Standard Time
PT pacific time
PTIC Patent and Trademark Institute of Canada

PTO please turn over
PV par value
PX private exchange

Q

QB Queen's Bench
QC Queen's Counsel
QDA quantity discount agreement
QED quod erat demonstrandum (L., which was to be demonstrated)
qtr quarter(ly)
qty quantity
qv quod vide (L., which see)

R

R&D research and development
RCL ruling case law
RD regional director
RE real estate
recd received
reg registered
reh den rehearing denied
req requisition
Rev reverend; revised
revd reversed
revg reversing
RFD rural free delivery
RFP request for proposal

RFQ request for quotation
RM resident magistrate
ROG receipt of goods
ROTC Reserve Officers' Training Corps
rpt report
R&R rest and recreation
RSVP respondez s'il vous plait (Fr., please reply)
Rt Hon Right Honorable
RTN registered trade name
Rt Rev Right Reverend

S

sa subject to approval
SALT Strategic Arms Limitation Talks
SANR subject to approval no risk
SAT Scholastic Aptitude Test
SB small bonds; statement of billing
SBA Small Business Administration
SC supreme court
SCM summary court martial
S Ct supreme court
SD same day; sight draft

sd sine die (L., without a day being named)
SDT subpoena duces tecum
SE stock exchange
SEATO South East Asia Treaty Organization
SEC Securities and Exchange Commission
sec secretary
secy secretary

BUSINESS AND THE LAW

SIA Securities Industry Association
SIPC Securities Investor Protection
 Corporation
SO seller's option
SOP standard operating procedure
SP stop payment
S&P systems and procedures
SS social security

SSE Spokane Stock Exchange
stat statute
stip stipulation
stk stock
stmt statement
sub opn subsequent opinion
supp supplement

T

TA tax agent
TB trial balance
TBA to be announced
TBW to be withheld
TC tax court; total cost
TECA Temporary Emergency Court of
 Appeals
Telex Teletypewriter Exchange
Temp temporary help/temporary per-

sonnel
TO table of organization
TOA table of authorities
TOC table of cases
trans transferred
treas treasurer
TSE Toronto Stock Exchange
TTY teletype
tx tax

U

UCC Universal Commercial Code
UI unemployment insurance
ui ut infra (L., as below)
UN United Nations
UPI United Press International
UPS United Parcel Service

US United States
us ut supra (L., as above)
USC under separate cover; United
 States Code
USCA United States Code Annotated

V

v versus
VA Veteran's Administration
VAR value added remarketer; value
 added reseller
VAT value added tax
vc valuation clause
vi vide infra (L., see below)
VIP very important person
viz videlicet (L., namely)

VO verbal order
vol volume
vou voucher
VP vice president
VPA value purchase agreement
vs versus
VSE Vancouver Stock Exchange
vt vote, voting
vv vice versa

W

wa   with average; will advise
WC   will call; without charge; working capital
wf   wrong font
whsle   wholesale
WI   when issued
wk   week
WOC   without compensation

wp   without prejudice; weather permitting
WPI   wholesale price index
wpm   words per minute
wr   with rights
WSE   Winnipeg Stock Exchange
wt   weight
ww   with warrants

X

X   an unknown
xcp   without coupon (NYSE)
xd   without dividend (NYSE)
xi   without interest (NYSE)
xn   ex new

xp   express paid
x per   without privileges
x rts   without rights (NYSE)
xw   without warrants

Y

Y   year
YB   yearbook
yld   yield
YMCA   Young Men's Christian Association
YMHA   Young Men's Hebrew Association

yr   year
YST   Yukon Standard Time
YTD   year to date
YMCA   Young Women's Christian Association
YWHA   Young Women's Hebrew Association

Z

Z   zone
ZIP   zone improvement plan

ZT   zone time

4

MEDICINE

(Medical Associations; Medical Conditions and Diseases; Treatments; Medicines; Prescriptions; Units of Measure; Table of Abbreviations of Common Vitamins)

A

A angstrom unit

a absent; absolute; absorbant; accommodation; acetum; acid; acidity; allergist; allergy; alpha; ampere; angstrom unit; annum (L., year); anode; answer; ante (L., before); aorta; aqueous; area; argon; artery; asymmetric; asymmetry; atria; atrophy; axial

AA achievement age; active assisted; Alcoholics Anonymous; automobile accident

aaa amalgam

AACIA American Association for Clinical Immunology and Allergy

AACP American Association of Colleges of Pharmacy

AACR American Association for Cancer Research

AACT American Association for Clinical Urologists

AADS American Association of Dental Schools

AAF ascorbic acid factor

AAFP American Academy of Family Physicians

AAGP American Academy of General Practice

AAHGS American Association of Health Data Systems

AAHPER American Association for Health, Physical Education and Recreation

AAL anterior axilary line

AAMC American Association of Medical Colleges

AAMIH American Association for Maternal and Infant Health

AAMRL American Association of Medical Records Librarians (now AMRA)

AAO American Association of Orthodontists; awake, alert and oriented

AAOP American Academy of Oral Pathology

AAP American Academy of Peridontology

AAPM American Academy of Physicists in Medicine

AB aid to blind; asthmatic bronchitis

ab abort; abortion; ace bandage; active bilaterally; antibodies

ABC atomic, biological, and chemical

abd abdomen, abdominal

abdom abdomen, abdominal

ABPM American Board of Preventive Medicine

ABR absolute bed rest

ABS acute brain syndrome; American Biological Society

abs absent; absolute

abs fed absante febre (L., absence of fever)

abst abstract

abt about; abstract

AC adrenal cortex; air conduction; alternating current; ante cibum (L., before meals)

ac acute

ACA American Chiropractic Association; anterior cerebral artery; anterior communicating aneurysms; anterior coronary artery

acad academy

acc accelerate; accelerated; acceleration; accommodation

accel accelerate; accelerated; acceleration

ACE mixture of alcohol, chloroform, and ether

acet acetone

ACh acetylcholine

AChe acetylcholinesterase

ACF accessory clinical findings

ACH adrenalcortical hormone

ACI acute coronary insufficiency

ACO alert, cooperative and oriented

ACP American College of Physicians

ACR American College of Radiology

ACS American College of Surgeons; antireticular cytotoxic serum

act active

ACTH adrenocorticotrophic hormone

AD adult disease; average deviation

ADA American Dental Association; American Diabetic Association; American Dietetic Association

ADAMHA Alcohol, Drug Abuse and Mental Health Administration

ADC aid to dependent children

addict addiction

adeq adequate

ADH antidiuretic hormone

adh adhesions

adhes adhesive

adj adjacent; adjoining; adjunct; adjusting

ADL activities of daily living

adm administration; administrator; admission; admit

ADMR adult minimum daily requirement

ADP adenosine diphosphate

ADPL average daily patient load

ADR accepted dental remedies

adren adrenalin

ADS antidiuretic substance

ADT adenosine triphosphate

ADW assault with a deadly weapon

ae aetatis (L., age, aged)

AES American Encephalographic Society; American Epidemiological Society

aet aetatis (L., age, aged)

aetat aetatis (L., age, aged)

AF acid fast; adult female; Arthritis Foundation; audio-frequency; auricular fibrillation

AFB acid-fast bacillus; American Foundation for the Blind

AFDC Aid to Families with Dependent Children

affil affiliated

AFIP Armed Forces Institute of Pathology

AFL artificial limb

AG against gravity

Ag antigen

AGA accelerated growth area

AGCT Army General Classification Test

agcy agency

agglut agglutination

aggrav aggravate; aggravation

agt agent

AHA American Heart Association; American Hospital Association

AHD acute heart disease

AHF American Hospital Formulary; antihemophilic globulin

AHG antihuman globulin

AHN assistant head nurse

AI accidentally incurred; artificial insemination

AIBS American Institute of Biological Sciences

AID acute infectious disease; artificial insemination by donor

AIDS acquired immune deficiency syndrome

AIH artificial insemination by husband

AJ ankle jerk

AK above knee

alb albumin

alc alcohol, alcoholic

ALG   antilymphocyte globulin
algy   allergy
align   alignment
alk   alkaline
ALS   amyotrophic lateral sclerosis; anti-
lymphocyte serum
alt   alternate; altitude
ALTS   acute lumbar traumatic sprain
alv   alveolar
AM   adult male
am   ammeter
AMA   against medical advice; American
Medical Association
amb   ambulance; ambulatory
AMEDS   Army Medical Corps
AMI   acute myocardial infarction
amp   amperage; ampule; amputation
amt   amount
AMR   alternate motion rate
AMRA   American Medical Records
Association
AMS   auditory memory span
AMSC   Army Medical Specialist Corps
AMT   American Medical Technologists
AMVET   American Veteran World
War II
ANA   American Nurse's Association
anal   analgesic; analysis
ANI   accute nerve irritation
ANRI   accute nerve root irritation
ANS   autonomic nervous system
AOM   Artrium Obstetricus Magister
(L., master of obstetric art)
AP   after parturation; analytical psy-
chology; anatomy and physiology; aor-
tic pulmonary; apothecary
A&P   anterior and posterior
APA   American Physiotherapy Associa-
tion; American Psychiatric Association
APHA   American Public Health Associa-
tion
Apoth   apothecary
app   apparatus; apparently; appendix;
application; appliance; appointment
approx   approximately
appy   appendectomy
AR   admitting room
ARC   American Red Cross
AROM   active range of motion
ARPT   American Registry of Physical
Therapists
ART   accredited record technician
art   artery; artificial
arth   arthritis
artic   articular
artif   artificial
art insem   artificial insemination
AS   aqueous suspension; arterioscle-
rosis
ASA   American Society of Anesthesiol-
ogists; American Standards Association
asap   as soon as possible
assist   assistant
assn   association
assoc   associate, associated, association
asth   asthma
asw   artificially sweetened
asx   asymptomatic
asym   asymmetrical
AT   achievement test; adjunctive
therapy; air temperature
atm   atmosphere, atmospheric
at no   atomic number
ATP   adenosine triphosphate
atr   atrophy
at vol   atomic volume
at wt   atomic weight
AU   angstrom unit
aud   auditory
aur   auricle
auric   auricle; auricular
aux   auxilary
AV   air velocity; arteriovascular;
average
A&W   alive and well
AZT   Ascheim-Zondek test

B

B   bacillus; barometric; base; behavior;
bicuspid; born
BA   blood alcohol; boric acid; bronchial
asthma
bact   bacteria, bacterial, bacteriology
bal   balance

BAO bachelor of arts in obstetrics
bar barometric
Barb barbituate
bas basilar
BBA born before arrival
BBB blood-brain barrier
BBT basal body temperature
BC bachelor of chemistry
BCP birth control pills
BD birth date
BDS bachelor of dental surgery
BDSc bachelor of dental science
bef before
beg begin
beh behavior
benz benzedrine
bet between
bev beverage
BF body fat
BHA butylated hydroxyanisole
BHL biological half life
BHT butylated hydroxytoluene
BI bodily injury; body injury
BIB brought in by
bio biology
biochem biochemistry
Bk biochemistry

BL bleeding; blood; blood loss
BM bachelor of medicine; basal metabolism; bowel movement
BMR basal metabolic rate
BMT bachelor of medical technology
BNDD Bureau of Narcotics and Dangerous Drugs
BO body odor
BOD biochemical oxygen demand; biological oxygen demand
BOT botanical; botany
BP birth place; blood pressure; bed pan; boiling point
BR bathroom; bed rest
Br breathe
Bronch bronchitis
BS bachelor of science; blood sugar
BSN bachelor of science in nursing
BT body temperature; brain tumor
BTW back to work
BUS Bartholin, urethra and Skene's
BV blood volume
BVR Bureau of Vocational Rehabilitation
BW bacteriological warfare; biological warfare; birthweight; body weight

C

C calorie; carbohydrate; cardiac; cast; cathode; Caucasian; Celsius; centigrade; central; certified; cervical; chest; coefficient; complex; compound; constant; coulomb (unit of electricity); current
CA cancer, carcinoma; cathode; chronological age
CAMSI Canadian Association of Medical Students and Interns
canc cancel, cancellation
CAOP Canadian Association of Occupational Therapy
cap capsule
CAPIS Canadian Association of Plastic Surgery
CAR Canadian Association of Radiologists; conditioned avoidance response

carbo carbohydrates
card cardiac
CARDE Canadian Armament Research and Development Establishment
CARE Cooperative for American Relief for Everyone
CARS Canadian Arthritis and Rheumatism Society
CAS Children's Aid Society
CAT child's apperception test; computed axial tomography; computerized axial tomography
cath catheter
CAT scan computer-assisted tomography scan
CAUSN Canadian Association of University Schools of Nursing

CAVD completion, arithmetic, vocabulary, and direction test
CB bachelor of surgery
Cb columbrium
CBC complete blood count
CBR chemical bacteriological and radiological
CBS chronic brain syndrome
CC chief complaint; coefficient of correlation; commission certified; common cold; craniocervical; current complaint
cc cubic centimeter
CCE Council on Chiropractic Education
CCL critical condition list
CCS Canadian Cancer Society; Crippled Children's Service
ccs cubic centimeters
CCU cardiac care unit; coronary care unit; critical care unit
CD childhood disease; contagious disease
CDA Canadian Dental Association
CDC Center for Disease Control (formerly Communicable Disease Center)
CDRF Canadian Dental Research Foundation
CEC Council for Exceptional Children
CER conditioned emotion response
CF case file; cystic fibrosis
cf/m cubic feet per minute
cg centigram
CGS centimeter-gram-second
ChB bachelor of surgery
char characteristic
CHD childhood diseases; coronary heart disease
ChD doctor of surgery
chem chemical; chemistry
CHF congestive heart failure
chg change
chl chloride
chlor chloroform
ChM master of surgery
CHO carbohydrate
chol cholesterol
CHP child psychiatry
chr chronic
CIC crisis intervention clinic
CICU cardiac intensive care unit
circ circulatory
CL clinic; close; closure; critical list

CLML current list of medical literature
CLO cod liver oil
CM master of surgery
cm centimeter
CMA Canadian Medical Association; certified medical assistant; county medical association
CMBES Canadian Medical and Biological Engineering Society
CMHA Canadian Mental Health Association
CMS circulation, motion and sensation
CMU complex motor unit
CN circulating nurse; cranial nerves
CNE chronic nervous exhaustion
CNS central nervous system
CO central office; certified orthotist; check out
coag coagulate, coagulation
COH carbohydrate
comm common; communicable
comp compound
compl complaint; complete; completed
CONA Canadian Orthopedic Nurses Association
CONELRAD control of electromagnetic radiation
cong congestion
cons consult, consultation, consultant
const constant
cont contagious, contagion
contd continued
COR custodian of records
CP certified prosthesist
cp child psychiatrist, child psychiatry; child psychologist; child psychology; closing pressure; constant pressure; candle power; compare
CPA Canadian Psychological Association
CPE complete physical examination
CPH certificate of public health
CPHA Canadian Public Health Association
cpm counts per minute
CPR cardio pulmonary resuscitation
cps cycles per second
CPX complete physical examination
CR clinical records; conditioned reflex; conditioned response
CRA Canadian Rheumatism Association

CRCC Canadian Red Cross Committee
CRD chronic respiratory disease
CRL certified record librarian
CRT cathode ray tube
CS Cesarean section; case; chief of staff; conscious; cycles per second
C sect Cesarean section
CSF Canadian Schizophrenia Foundation; cerebro spinal fluid
CSPH Canadian Society of Hospital Pharmacists
CST convulsive shock therapy
CT continue treatment
CTA Canadian Tuberculosis Association
C₂H₃OH alcohol
cu cubic centimeter

cu ft cubic foot
cu in cubic inch
cult culture
cu m cubic meter
cu mm cubic millimeter
CV cardiovascular; cervical vertibra; coefficient of variation; cardiac volume
CVD cardiovascular disease
CVMA Canadian Veterinary Medical Association
CVP central venous pressure
CV status cardiovascular status
CW chemical warfare; continous wave
CWP childbirth without pain
Cx cervix
cyl cylindrical
cytol cytology

D

D daughter; day; dead; deceased; degree; density; dermatology; dermatologist; deuterium; deviation; dextros; diagnosis; diameter; Diathermy; disease; dorsal; duration
D/A date of admission
dal decaliter
DAT differential aptitude test
D/B date of birth
Db decibel
dbl double
DC diagnostic center; direct current; doctor of chiropractic
D&C dilatation and curettage
DDS doctor of dental surgery
DDSc doctor of dental science
dec deceased; decimeter
def deficiency; deficient
Dem demerol
dent dental; dentist; dentistry
derm dermatologist; dermatology
detox detoxification
dev develop; development; deviate; deviation
df degrees of freedom
DHEW Department of Health, Education and Welfare
DI date of injury

dia diathermy
diab diabetes, diabetic
diag diagonal; diagram
diff difference
dil dilate; dilated; dilation; dilute; diluted; dilution
dim diminished
disp dispensary; dispense
dist distilled
dkg decagram
dkl decaliter
dkm dekameter
DM doctor of medicine
DMD doctor of dental medicine
DMS doctor of medical science
DMSO dimethyl sulfoxide
DNA deoxyribonucleic acid
DO doctor of osteopathy; doctor of optometry
DOA date of admission; dead on arrival
DP doctor of pharmacy; doctor of podiatry
DPH department of public health
DPM doctor of podiatric medicine
DPT diptheria, pertussis, tetanus
DR diagnostic radiology
Dr doctor

DS doctor of science
DSC doctor of surgical chiropody
DTs delirium tremens

DVM doctor of veterinary medicine
DWI driving while intoxicated
dz dozen

E

E einsteinium; electromotive force; enema; enzyme; experiment
EC enteric coated
ECF extended care facility
ECG electrocardiogram
ECT electroconvulsive therapy
EEG electroencephalogram
EENT eye, ear, nose and throat
EM electron microscope
EMF electromotive force
EMT emergency medical technician
ENT ear, nose and throat
EOP emergency out patient
epil epilepsy; epileptic

ER emergency room
ESB electrical stimulation of the brain
ESP extra sensory perception
EST electroshock therapy
ESU electrostatic unit
EW emergency ward
ex exercise
exc excellent
excr excrete; excreted; excretion
exp experiment; expiration; expose; exposure
expl explain
ext exterior; external; extract; extreme
extrem extremity

F

F Fahrenheit; farad; female; fluid; fluorine
f fluid; formula; fracture
FA fatty acid; first aid; folic acid
FACD Fellow of American College of Dentists
FACHA Fellow of American College of Hospital Administrators
FACP Fellow of American College of Physicians; Fellow of American College of Pathologists
FAMA Fellow of American Medical Association
FAPA Fellow of American Psychiatric Association
FAPHA Fellow of American Public Health Association

FAO Food and Agricultural Organization
FD focal distance
FDA Food and Drug Administration
Fe iron
feb fever
FH family history
FICS Fellow of International College of Surgeons
FI focal length
fl oz fluid ounce
FMH family medical history
FOP forensic pathology
fpm feet per minute
fps feet per second; foot pound second; frames per second
frac fracture
FTND full term normal delivery

G

G   glucose
g   gram
GA   general anesthesia
gal   gallon
GATB   government aptitude test battery
gen   genetics
geron   gerontology
GG   gamma globulin
GH   general health; growth hormone
GI   gastrointestinal
G/L   grams per liter
glu   glucose
GM   general medicine
gm   gram
gm/l   grams per liter

GMA   gross motor activities
GMS   general medicine and surgery
GMW   gram molecular weight
GNC   general nursing counsel
GP   general paralysis; general practice; general practitioner
GPM   general preventive medicine
GR   gamma roentgen
gr   grain; gravity; gravida (L., pregnant)
GRAS   generally recognised as safe
gr wt   gross weight
GS   general surgeon
GSR   galvanic skin response
GT   group therapy
GTT   glucose tolerance test
Gyn   gynecologist; gynecology

H

H   height; heroin;
HA   headache
HB   hemoglobin
HBD   has been drinking
HBO   hyperbaric oxygen
HBP   high blood pressure
HC   hemoglobin concentration; home care
HCL   hydrochloric acid
HDL   high density lipoprotein
hem   hemorrhage; hemorhoid
hematol   hematologist; hematology
hemo   hemophilia
HENT   head, eyes, ears, nose and throat
HEW   Health, Education and Welfare (U.S. government department)
HF   heart failure; high frequency
hf   half
HGH   human growth hormone
HH   hard of hearing
HI   hospital insurance
HIS   Haptic Intelligence Scale
hist   histologist; histology

HL   hearing loss
HMO   Health Maintenance Organization
HN   head nurse
HOH   water (hydrogen–oxygen–hydrogen)
HOPE   Health Opportunity for People Everywhere
HOPI   history of present illness
HP   high potency; high pressure
HPI   history of present illness
HR   heart rate
hr   hour
H₂O   water
HV   hospital visit
hyd   hydration; hydraulic
hydro   hydrotherapy
HSMHA   Health Services and Mental Health Administration
hyg   hygiene
hypo   hypodermic
hys   hysteria; hysterical; hysterectomy
Hz   hertz

I

I   index; internist
IC   intensive care
ICF   intracellular fluid
ICRC   International Committee of the Red Cross
ICT   insulin coma therapy
ICU   intensive care unit
ID   identification
IDA   iron deficiency anemia
IF   intermediate frequency
IH   infectious hepatitis
IM   internal medicine
IMA   Industrial Medicine Association
IME   independent medical examination; independent medical examiner
immun   immune, immunize, immunization, immunity
inc   incomplete; inconclusive
incr   increase; increased; increment
IH   industrial hygiene
inf   infancy; infant; infantile; infarction; infect; infected; infection; infectious; infirmary; infusion; insulin
insol   insoluable
insp   inspect; inspection
inst   institute; institution; institutional
IOC   interne on call
IP   in patient
IPMR   Institute of Physical Medicine and Rehabilitation
ips   inches per second
IQ   intelligence quotient
IRM   Institute of Rehabilitational Medicine
IS   isolate; isolation
ISC   International Society of Chemotherapy
IST   insulin shock therapy
IT   industrial therapy; intensive therapy
ITT   insulin tolerance test
IU   immunizing unit; international unit; intra uterine
IUD   intra uterine device
IV   intervertebral; intravenous

J

J   joule
JAMA   Journal of the American Medical Association
JCAH   Joint Commission on Accreditation of Hospitals
JRC   Junior Red Cross

K

K   constant; Kelvin scale; kilo
KC   kilocycle
K Cal   kilocalorie
KCL   potassium chloride
Kcps   kilocycles per second
Kev   thousand electron volts
kg   kilogram (1,000 grams)
Kg cal   kilogram calorie
kgm   kilogram
kg-m   kilogram meter
kgps   kilograms per second
kilo   metric prefix meaning 1,000
Kl   kiloliter
Km   kilometer
kmps   kilometers per second
kv   kilovolt
kva   kolovolt ampere
kvp   kilovolts peak
kw-h   kilowatt hour

L

L   Lambert (unit of light); liter; lumbar
LA   local anesthesia
Lab   laboratory
lac   laceration
lact   lactate; lactating; lactation
lb   pounds
LBP   low blood pressure
LBW   low birth weight
LD   lethal dose
LDL   low density lipoprotein
LG   large

Li   ligament
Liq   liquid
LP   latent period
lpm   liters per minute
LPN   licensed practical nurse
LSD   lysergic acid diethylamide
LV   left ventrical
LVN   licensed vocational nurse
LX   local irradiation
Lymph   lymphocyte

M

M   male; meter(s); malignent; minimum
MA   menstral age; mental age
MABP   mean arterial blood pressure
MAC   macerate; maximum allowable concentration
mag   magnification
MAT   manual arts therapist
max   maximum
MBP   mean blood pressure
Mc   millicurie
MCAT   Medical College Admission Test
mcg   microgram
MCT   mean circulation time
MD   medicinae doctor (L., doctor of medicine); medical department; muscular dystrophy
MDR   minimum daily requirement
MDS   master of dental surgery
ME   medical examiner
Me   methyl
Med   medical; medicine
MEDLARS   Medical Literature Analysis and Retrieval System
MEF   mean effective pressure
mega   one million
memb   membrane
mev   million electron volts
mfd   microfarad
mg   milligram
MH   marital history

MHA   Mental Health Association
MHB   maximum hospital benefit
mHg   millimeters of mercury
micro   one-millionth
milli   one-thousandth
min   minimum
ml   milliliter
mmm   micromillimeter
MMPI   Minnesota Multiphasic Personality Inventory
mmpp   millimeters partial pressure
MN   midnight
M&N   morning and night
MO   mineral oil; month
MOM   milk of magnesia
MOR Dict   moris dicto (L., in the manner directed)
MOR SOL   more solito (L., in the usual way)
MP   modo prescripto (L., as directed)
MPC   maximum permissible concentration
MPH   master of public health
MR   mental retardation
mr   milliroentgen
MRD   minimum reacting dose
MS   master of science; master of surgery; morphine sulphate; multiple sclerosis
msec   millisecond

MSG   monosodium glutimate
MSN   master of science in nursing
MT   empty; medical technologist; medical technology; more than
MTD   maximum tolerated dose
MTT   mean transit time
mU   milliunit

mu   micron
MV   minute volume
mv   millivolt
MW   molecular weight
mw   microwave
my   myopia
My G   myasthenia gravis

N

N   nasal; nerve; normal
NA   nurse's aide
NAMH   National Association for Mental Health
NB   newborn
nb   nota bene (L., note well)
NBM   nothing by mouth
NBW   normal birth weight
NC   no change
N/C   no complaints
NCA   National Council on Alcoholism
ND   neonatal deaths; new drugs; no date
NE   no effect; not examined
NED   no evidence of disease
Neg   negative
Neuro   neurological
NF   National Formulary
NI   no information
NIA   no information available
NIAID   National Institute of Allergy and Infectious Diseases
NIDA   National Institute on Drug Abuse
NIGMS   National Institute of General Medical Sciences
NIH   National Institute of Health
NIMH   National Institute of Mental Health
NIL   nill (L., none)

NK   not known
NLM   National Library of Medicine
NND   neonatal death
NOC   nocte (L., night)
Non Rep   non repetatur (L., do not repeat)
NOPHN   National Organization for Public Health Nursing
norm   normal
np   neuropsychiatric
NPH   neutral protamine Hagedorn
NPN   nonprotein nitrogen
NPO   null peros (L., nothing by mouth)
NPT   normal pressure and temperature
NR   no refill
NS   nervous system
N/S   normal saline
NSC   no significant change
NSPB   National Society for the Prevention of Blindness
NsQ   not sufficient quantity
NSS   normal saline solution
NSU   nonspecific urethritis
NT   not tested
NTA   National Tuberculosis Association
NTP   normal temperature and pressure
Nv   naked vision
N&V   nausea and vomiting

O

O   orally; orderly
OAA   old age assistance
OAS   old age security

OASI   old age and survivors insurance
Ob   obstetrics
OBG   obstetrics and gynecology

MEDICINE

OBS obstetrics
obs observe; observer; observation
OC oral contraceptive
OCC occasional
OD overdose; one a day
O&E observation and examination
OG obstetrics and gynecology
OGTT oral glucose tolerance test
OHDS Office of Human Development Services
OJ orange juice
Ol oil
OM omni mane (L., every morning)
Omn Bih omni bihora (L., every hour)
Omn Noct omni nocte (L., every night)

ON omni nocte (L., every night)
OOB out of bed
OP operation; out patient
OPC out patient clinic
OPH opthamology
OPS out patient service
OPV oral poliovaccine
OR operating room
org organic
ORS orthopedic surgery
ORTH orthopedics; orthopedic surgery
OT occupational therapy
OTC over the counter
OTOL otology
OW out of wedlock
OZ ounce

P

P plasma; post (L., after)
PA psychoanalyst
P&A percussion and auscultation
PABA para-aminobenzoic acid
PAM penicillin aluminum monostearate
PAP smear Papanicolaou smear
PAR post anesthesia room
Para-2 two pregnancies
Path pathology
Pb phenobarbitol
PBI protein bound iodine
PBO placebo
PC post cibum (L., after meals)
PCN penicillin
pCO₂ pressure of carbon dioxide
PD pediatrics
PEN penicillin
PENT Pentothal™
Per by; for each; through
PER OS per os (L., by mouth, through mouth)
Pg pregnant
PH past history
pH presence of hydrogen ions (measure of acidity)
Phar pharmacy
Phar D doctor of pharmacy
PhC pharmaceutical chemist

PHS Public Health Service
PI personal injury; preliminary investigation; present illness
pico one-trillionth
PKU phenylketonuria
PM post meridian (L., in the afternoon); post mortem
PMD private medical doctor
PMS pre menstrual syndrome; post menopausal syndrome
PN practical nurse
PNC penicillin
PO per os (L., by mouth)
POC post operative care
pOH concentration of Hydroxyl
Polio poliomyelitis
Pos positive
Post posterior
Post Op post operative
PP post partum
ppm parts per million
PRC packed red cells
Pre preliminary
Preg pregnant
Pre Op preoperative
Prep preparation
PRN pro re nata (L., as the occasion arises)

90

Prog prognosis
Prox proximal
Ps prescription
P/S poly unsaturated
psi pounds per square inch
PSY psychiatry
PT physical therapy
PTA prior to admission
PTB prior to birth

PU peptic ulcer
PUFA polyunsaturated fatty acids
Pul pulmonary
Pulv pulvis (L., powder)
PV plasma volume
Px physical examination
Pyd pyridine
PZI protamine zinc insulin

Q

Q quantity
QAM quisque mane (L., every morning)
QD quisque dies (L., every day)
QH quisque horae (L., every hour)
QID quater in dies (L., four times daily)
QL quantum libet (L., as much as desired)
QNS quantity not sufficient
QOD quisque alius dies (L., every other day)

QP quantum placeat (L., at will)
QPM quisque nocte (L., every night)
QQ quisque (L., each)
QQH quisque quarta hora (L., every four hours)
qs quantity sufficient
Qt quart; quiet
quar quarter, quarterly
qv quod vide (L., which see)

R

R radioactive; rectal; respiration; right; roentgen
RAD radial; radiation
RAI radioactive iodine; radio-immunoassay
RBC red blood cells
RBF renal blood flow
RCC red cell count
RCPSC Royal College of Physicians and Surgeons of Canada
RCS Royal College of Surgeons
RCT Rorschach Content Test
R&D research and development
RDA recommended daily allowance
RDS respiratory distress syndrome
RE retinol equivalent
ref reference
regen regenerate, regeneration
Rep repetatur (L., let it be repeated)

Res research
Resp respiratory
RF rheumatic fever
RH relative humidity
Rh Rhesus factor
rhm roentgen per hour at one meter
RI refractive index
RIU radioactive-iodine uptake
RLS Ringers lactated solution
RMV respiratory minute volume
RN registered nurse
RNA ribonucleic acid
RO routine order
ROM range of motion
rot rotation
RP registered pharmacist
rpm revolutions per minute
RPT registered physical therapist
RQ respiratory quotient

RR radiation response; recovery room
R&R rest and recuperation
RRL registered record librarian
RSH Royal Society for the Promotion of Health

RT radiation therapy
RTD retarded
RTN return
Rx prescription

S

S sacral; soluble; surgeon; surgery
SA surface area
Sa samarium
SAH subarachnoid hemorrhage
sanit sanitary; sanitation
sat saturated
sat sol saturated solution
SB sirum bilirubin
SBE subacute bacterial endocarditis
SBP systolic blood pressure
SC special care
Sc scapula
sc subcutaneous
SCB strictly confined to bed
SCD service connected disability
Sci science; scientific
SCU special care unit
SDM standard deviation of the mean
SE standard error
sec second; secondary
sem semen; seminal
sep separate; separated; separation
ser serial; series; service
serv services
SEV severe
SF spinal fluid
SFC spinal fluid count
SM symptom
SI soluble insulin
SIC surgical intensive care
SID sudden infant death

SIG sigmoidoscopy
SMR somnolent metabolic rate
SN student nurse
SNM Society of Nuclear Medicine
SNS sympathetic nervous system
SOB short of breath
SOC sequential oral contraceptive
SOD superoxide dismutase
Sol solution
Solv solvent
SOPS si opus sit (L., if it is necessary)
SPBI serum protein bound iodine
Spc specimen
SPCA Society for the Prevention of Cruelty to Animals
SPCC Society for the Prevention of Cruelty to Children
Sp Gr specific gravity
SPR Society for Physical Research
Sq square
ST survival time
Staph staphylococcus
Strep streptococcus
SUP superficial; superior
supp suppository
SVC superior vena cava
SW social worker
Sx excess; symptoms
SYM symmetrical
Syr syrum
syst system; systolic

T

T temperature; time; total; trace; transverse
Tab tablet

TAH total abdominal hysterectomy
TAT tetinus antitoxin
TB tuberculosis

TBF   total body fat
TBLC   term birth living child
TBV   total blood volume
TBW   total body weight
TBX   total body irradiation
TC   tetracycline; tissue culture; total capacity; total cholesterol
TD   typhoid dysentery
TE   trial and error
Te   tetanus
tech   technical
term   terminal
TF   tuning fork
TH   thyroid hormone
Th   thoracic; thorax
THC   tetrahydrocannabinol
Ther   therapy

TL   tubal ligation
Tl   thallium
TMV   tobacco mosaic virus
TO   temperature, oral
tr   trace; tremor
TR   temperature, rectal; theraputic radiology
TQ   tourniquet
trans   transverse
TRI   total response index
TS   test solution; thoracic surgery
TSH   thyroid stimulating hormone
TSP   total serum proteins
tsp   teaspoonful
TU   toxic unit
TV   total volume
TW   tap water
TX   traction

U

U   unit; unknown; urology
UA   urine analysis
UBI   ultraviolet blood irradiation
U&C   urethral and cervical; usual and customary
UCD   usual childhood diseases
UCS   uncontrolled stimulus
UCT   urea clearance test
UCV   uncontrolled variable
UG   urogenital
UH   upper half
UHF   ultra high frequency

UK   unknown
UN   urea nitrogen
UNK   unknown
UQ   upper quadrant
UR   urine
Urol   urological, urologist, urology
USP   United States Pharmacopoeia
USPHS   United States Public Health Service
UTI   urinary tract infection
UV   ultraviolet

V

V   vein; volt; voltmeter; volume
VA   visual acuity
Vac   vacuum
Vacc   vaccination
Vag   vagina
Var   variation
VB   viable birth

VC   vital capacity
VCC   vasoconstrictor center
VCG   vector cardiogram
VCS   vasoconstrictor substance
VD   venereal disease
VDA   visual discriminatory acuity
VDRL   venereal disease research laboratory

MEDICINE

Vent ventricular
Vet veteran; veterinary
VHF very high frequency
VIP very important patient
Vit vitamin
VLDL very low density lipoprotein
VLF very low frequency
VM vasomotor; vestibular membrane; voltmeter
VNA Visiting Nurses Association

VO verbal order
Vol volume; volumetric; voluntary; volunteer
VP vapor pressure; venous pressure
vps vibrations per second
VR vocal resonance
VRI virum respiratory infection
VS veterinary surgeon; volumetric solution
VU volume unit
VW vessel wall

W

W water; weight; width
WB whole blood
WBC white blood cells
WBR whole body radiation
WC water closet (bathroom); wheel chair; white cell
WD wet dressing
WF white female
WHO World Health Organization
WIA wounded in action

Wk weak; week
WL waiting list; wave length
WM white male
WN well nourished
WO without
Wo written order
WP wet pack
WR Wasserman reaction
WS water soluble
Wt weight

X

XM cross match
XR X-ray

XRT X-ray technician

Y

Y year
yd yard

YOB year of birth
Yr year

Z

Z zero; zone
zool zoological, zoology

ZPG zero population growth

TABLE OF ABBREVIATIONS OF
COMMON VITAMINS

A1	Retinol	**D**	Calciferol
A2	Dehydroretinol	**D2**	Ergocalciferol
B1	Thiamine	**D3**	Cholecalciferol
B2	Riboflavin	**E**	Alpha tocopherol
B3	Niacin	**F**	Fatty acids
B5	Pantothenic acid	**G**	Riboflavin (also called B2)
B6	Pyridoxine	**H**	Biotin
B12	Cobalamin	**K1**	Phytonadione
B13	Orotic acid	**K2**	Menaquinone
B15	Pangamic acid	**K3**	Menadione
B17	Laetril	**M**	Folic acid
C	Ascorbic acid		

5

INDUSTRY AND SCIENCE

(Chemistry; Metallurgy; Engineering; Architecture; Nautical Terms; Meteorology)

A

A ace; angstrom unit; argon

a acre; alpha; alphanumeric; ampere; anode; anterior

AAAS American Association for the Advancement of Science

AAERR Aerophysics and Aerospace Engineering Research Report

AAG Association of American Geographers

AALAS American Association for Laboratory Animal Science

AAPS Automated Astronomic Positioning System

AAS atomic absorption spectrophotometry; atomic absorption spectroscopy

AASE Department of Aerophysics and Aerospace Engineering

AATT American Association for Textile Technology

abl ablative

abs absolute

abstr abstract

AC alternating current

ACA Association of Consulting Architects

ACACT Associate Committee on Air-Cushion Technology (Canada)

ACDPS Automated Cartographic, Drafting and Photogrammetric System

ACGIH American Conference of Government Industrial Hygienists

ACEC American Consulting Engineers Council

ACEMB Annual Conference on Engineering in Medicine and Biology

ACGR Associate Committee on Geotechnical Research (Canada)

ACIL American Council of Independent Laboratories

ACMC Agricultural and Construction Machinery Council

ACME Association of Consulting Management Engineers

ACRE Advanced Chemical Rocket Engineering Program

ACS American Chemical Society; Association of Consultant Surveyors; Association of Consulting Scientists

actg acting

ADF automatic direction finder

adj adjustment

AE agricultural engineer

AEC Atomic Energy Commission

AES artificial earth satellite

AETE aerospace engineering test establishment

AF audio frequency

AFC automatic frequency control

aff affirmative

AGC   automatic gain control
agr   agriculture
agric   agriculture
AGS   acoustic guidance sonar
ah   amphere-hour
AIA   Abrasive Industries Association; American Institute of Architects
AIAA   American Institute of Aeronautics and Astronautics
AIC   American Institute of Chemists
AIChE   American Institute of Chemical Engineers
AIDE   Automated Integrated Design and Engineering
AIDS   Advanced Impact Drilling System
AIEE   American Institute of Electrical Engineers
AIHA   American Industrial Hygienists Association
AIMMPE   American Institute of Mining, Metallurgical and Petroleum Engineers
alc   alcohol
alg   algebra
alk   alkaline
alky   alkalinity
alt   alternate; alternative; alternator; altitude
AM   amplitude modulation
am   ante meridium
AMCAP   Advanced Microwave Circuit Analysis Programme
AMOS   Acoustic Meteorological Oceanographic Survey
amp   ampere
amp hr   ampere hour
AMRL   Applied Mechanics Research Laboratory
AMTDA   Agricultural Machinery and Tractor Dealers Association
AMU   atomic mass unit
an   annum
anal   analogy; analysis
analy   analytic
anhyd   anhydrous
anon   anonymous
Ant   antrium
ant   antenna
anthro   anthropology
anthrop   anthropology
antilog   antilogarithm
AOU   apparent oxygen utilization

AP   arithmetic progression
APL   applied physics laboratory
app   apparatus; appendix; application
appl   applied
approx   approximate, approximately
appt   appoint, appointment
AQ   accomplishment quotient; achievement quotient
aq   aqueous
Ar   argon
arch   architecture
archeol   archeology
Arg   Argyle
arg   argent
arith   arithmetic
ARLIS   Arctic Research Lab Island
ART   airborne radiation thermometer
AS   Academy of Science
As   altostratus
ASA   American Standards Association; American Statistical Association
ASCE   American Society of Civil Engineers
asgd   assigned
asgmt   assignment
ASME   American Society of Mechanical Engineers
ASL   American Society for Oceanography
ASR   airport surveillance radar; air-sea rescue
ASSESS   analytical studies of surface effects of submerged submarines
ASTM   American Society for Testing Materials
astrol   astrology
astron   astronomy
ASW   antisubmarine warfare
ASWEPS   antisubmarine warfare environmental prediction system
at   airtight; atomic
atm   atmosphere; atmospheric
at no   atomic number
ATP   adenosine triphosphate
attrib   attribute
at vol   atomic volume
at wt   atomic weight
AU   angstrom unit
aud   auditory
aug   augment
AUTEC   Atlantic Underwater Test and Evaluation Center

auth   authorized
aux   auxiliary
AV   audiovisual; authorized version
avg   average

AW   actual weight; all water
AWG   American wire gauge
ax   axiom
az   azimuth

B

B   brightness; bulb
b   bacillus
bact   bacteria, bacterial, bacteriology
bal   balance
bar   barometer, barometric
BArch   bachelor of architecture
bbl   barrel(s)
BC   bathyconductograph
BCG   bacillus-Calmette-Guerin
BChE   bachelor of chemical engineering
BCS   bachelor of commercial science
bd   barrels per day
bd ft   board foot
BE   bachelor of engineering
BEC   British Engineers Club
BEV   billion electron volts
BHN   brinell hardness number
BHP   brake horsepower
bio   biology
biochem   biochemistry
biol   biology, biological
BIOS   Biological Information Service
bl   bale
BlDGE   building engineer

bldr   builder
BM   basal metabolism; bench mark
bm   beam
BMEP   brake mean effective power
BMR   basal metabolic rate
BOD   biochemical oxygen demand
botan   botany, botanical
BP   blueprint; British Pharmacopoeia; British Petroleum
bp   boiling point
BPD   barrels per day
BPF   bottom pressure fluctuation
Br   British
br   brass
brl   barrel
BRS   Bibliographic Retrieval Service
BS   bachelor of science
BSA   bachelor of science in architecture
BT   bathythermograph
btry   battery
BTU   British thermal unit
bu   bushel
BWG   Birmingham wire gauge
bwo   backward wave oscillator

C

C   Celsius; centigrade; centum
c   candle; capacitance; carat; cathode; cycle
CA   chronological age
ca   circa
CAB   Civil Aeronautics Board
CABMA   Canadian Association of British Manufacturers and Agencies
CACA   Canadian Agricultural Chemicals Association

CAES   Canadian Agricultural Economics Society
CAG   Canadian Association of Geographers
CAI   Canadian Aeronautical Institute
cal   calories, caloric
calc   calculate, calculation, calculator
CAMESA   Canadian Military Electronics Standards Agency
canc   canceled; cancellation

CANCEE Canadian National Committee for Earthquake Engineering

CAN/TAP Canadian Technical Awareness Programme

CANWEC Canadian National Committee of the World Energy Conference

CAP Canadian Association of Physicists

cap capacity; capital; capsule

CART Canadian Amateur Radio Teletype Group

CAS Canadian Cooperative Applications Satellite; Chemical Abstracts Service

CASI Canadian Aeronautics and Space Institute

CATCC Canadian Association of Textile Colourists and Chemists

CAVU ceiling and visibility unlimited

Cb columbium

CBASF current bibliography for aquatic sciences and fisheries

CBS Canadian Biochemical Society

Cc cirrocumulus

cc cubic centimeter

CCA Canadian Chemical Association; Canadian Construction Association

CCAM Canadian Congress of Applied Mechanics

CCBDA Canadian Copper and Brass Development Association

CCITT Consultative Committee on International Telegraphy and Telephony

CCNDT Canadian Council for Non-Destructive Technology

CCPE Canadian Council of Professional Engineers

ccw counter clockwise

CD current density

cd cord

CDC Canadian Development Association

CDRA Canadian Drilling Research Association

CDRB Canadian Defence Research Board

CdS cadmium sulphide

CE chemical engineer; civil engineer; computer engineer

cem cement

CEMF counter electromotive force

cen central

cent centigrade

cert certified

CESA Canadian Engineering Standards Association

CESSS Council of Engineering and Scientific Society Secretaries (U.S. and Canada)

CFA Canadian Federation of Agriculture; Canadian Forestry Association

CFAP Canadian Association for the Advancement of Pharmacy

CFM cubic feet per minute

CFPMO Canadian Forces Project Management Office

CFSPL Canadian Forces Special Projects Laboratory

CFS cubic feet per second

CG center of gravity

cg centigram

CGA Canadian Gas Association

CGS Canadian Geotechnical Society

cgs centimeter-gram-second

ch chart

chem chemical; chemistry

chg charge

chron chronology

CHS Canadian Hydrographic Service

CI cast iron

ci cirrus

CIC Chemical Institute of Canada

CIM Canadian Institute of Mining

CIMM Canadian Institute of Mining and Metallurgy

CIPA Canadian Industrial Preparedness Association

CIPS Canadian Institute on Pollution Control

cir circular

CIS Canadian Institute of Surveying

CISP Canadian Institute of Surveying and Photogrammetry

CISTI Canadian Institute for Scientific and Technical Information

cl centiliter; class; classification; close

clin clinical

cm centimeter

CMA Chemical Manufacturers Association

CMCSA Canadian Manufacturers of Chemical Specialties Association

CMP Canadian Mineral Processors

CMRA Chemical Marketing Research Association

CNA Canadian Nuclear Association

CNS central nervous system

CODC Canadian Oceanographic Data Center

COIC Canadian Oceanographic Identification Center

coeff coefficient

col colored

colog cologarithm

comp comparative; compiler; compound

conc concentrate, concentrated

conch conchology

cond conductivity

conf conference

constr construction

cont control

contg containing

contr contract

corr correction

CORS Canadian Operational Research Society

cos cosine

COSMAT Committee on the Survey of Materials Science and Engineering

COSTED Committee on Science and Technology in Developing Countries

cot cotangent

CP candlepower; chemically pure

cpd compound

CPI Council of the Printing Industries of Canada

CPIC Canadian Police Information Centre

CPM cycles per minute

CPSA Consumer Products Safety Act

CPSC Consumer Products Safety Commission

cr cathode ray

CRESS Center for Research in Experimental Space Sciences (Canada)

CRGR Coalition for Responsible Genetic Research

CRIQ Centre de Recherche Industrielle du Quebec (Quebec Industrial Research Center)

CRM Centre de Recherches Mathematiques (Center for Mathematical Research, University of Montreal, Quebec)

CRS Communications Research Center

cryst crystalline

cs case

c/s cycles per second

CSA Canadian Standards Association

CSAE Canadian Society of Agricultural Engineering

CSCE Canadian Society of Chemical Engineers

CSChE Canadian Society for Chemical Engineering

CSCE Canadian Society of Civil Engineers

CSEE Canadian Society of Civil Engineering

CSFA Canadian Scientific Film Association

CSFE Canadian Society of Forest Engineers

CSGA Canadian Seed Growers Association

CSI Construction Specifications Institute

CSICC Canadian Steel Industries Construction Council

CSIN Chemical Substances Information Network

CSLATP Canadian Society of Landscape Architects and Town Planners

CSLO Canadian Scientific Liaison Office

CSLT Canadian Society of Laboratory Technologists

CSRS Cooperative State Research Service

CSSA Crop Science Society of America

CSSE Conference of State Sanitary Engineers

CSSS Canadian Soil Science Society

CST Central Standard Time

ctr center

cu cubic

cu ft cubic foot (or feet)

cu in cubic inch(es)

cum cumulative

CUMA Canadian Urethane Manufacturers Association

cu mi cubic mile(s)

cur current

cu yd cubic yard

CW commercial weight

cytol cytology

D

D diameter; dimension
d data; degree; density; distance; dyne
db decibel(s)
DBER Division of Biomedical and Environmental Research
dbl double
dbu decibel unit
DC decimal classification; direct current
DDI depth deviation indicator
DDT Dichlorodiphenytrichloroethane
dec decrease
deg degree(s)
dev deviation
DEW distant early warning
DF direction finder, directional finding
dg decigram(s)
DHQ mean diurnal high water inequality
diag diagonal; diagram
diam diameter
dil dilute
dim dimension; diminished
dis discharge
dkg decagram
dkl decaliter
dkm decameter
dks dekastere
dl deciliter
DLQ mean diurnal low water inequality
dm decimeter
DMAAC Defence Mapping Agency Aerospace Center
DMAHC Defence Mapping Agency Hydrographic Center

DME distance measuring equipment; Division of Mechanical Engineering
DNA deoxyribonucleic acid
dof degree of freedom
dom dominant
doz dozen
DP data processing; degree of polymerization; dew point; diametrical pitch
DPW Department of Public Works
dr drive
DRT dead reckoning tracer
DRV deep research vehicle
ds decistere
DSARC Defense Systems Acquisition Review Council
DSIR Department of Scientific and Industrial Research
DSRV deep submergence rescue vehicle
DSSP deep submergence systems project
DSSRG deep submergence systems research group
DST daylight saving time
dstn destination
DTG date time group
DUMS deep unmanned submersibles
dw dead weight
dwc dead weight capacity
dwg drawing
dwt dead weight tons
dyn dynamo
dynam dynamic
dz dozen

E

E east; Einsteinium; engineer
e erg
EAI Engineers and Architects Institute
ECG electrocardiogram
ecol ecology
ECRC Engineering College Research Council

ECS Electrochemical Society, Inc.
EE electrical engineer; errors expected
EEG electroencephalogram
EEI Edison Electric Institute
EEIB Environmental Engineering Intersociety Board
EF Engineering Foundation

eff effective
EHF extremely high frequency
EHP effective horsepower
EIA Electronic Industries Association
EIC Electronic Institute of Canada
EIRMA European Industrial Research Management Association
EJC Engineers Joint Council
EKG electrocardiogram
el elevation
elec electric, electrical, electricity
E Long east longitude
EM Engineer of Mines
Em electromagnetic
EMA electronic missile acquisition
EMBC European Molecular Biology Conference
EMBO European Molecular Biology

Organization
embryol embryology
EMF electromotive force
EMU electromagnetic unit
eng engine
EP extraction procedure
EPA Environmental Protection Agency
EPRI Electronic Power Research Institute
ERDA Energy Research and Development Administration
ESA European Space Agency
ESF European Science Foundation
ESOC European Space Operations Center
ESRO European Space Research Organization
EUP Environmental Use Permit

F

F Fahrenheit
f farad; force
FAA Federal Aviation Administration
FAAAS Fellow of the American Association for the Advancement of Science
fac facsimile
FAGS Fellow of the American Geographical Society
FAIA Fellow of the American Institute of Architects
FAO Food and Agriculture Organization
FAS Federation of American Scientists
fath fathom
fbm feet board measure
FCC Federal Communications Commission
FD Food and Drug Administration
fdy foundry
FEA Federal Energy Administration
FEO Federal Energy Office
FFDCA Federal Food, Drug and Cosmetic Act
FHSA Federal Hazardous Substances Act

FIEP Forest Industry Energy Program
FIFRA Federal Insecticide, Fungicide and Rodenticide Act
fl fluid
fl dr fluid dram
fl oz fluid ounce
flt flight
FM frequency modulation
fm fathom
fnp fusion point
FPC Federal Power Commission
FPRS Forest Products Research Society
FPS Fluid Power Society
fps feet per second; frames per second
FSP Federal Specifications Board
ft foot or feet
FTC Federal Trade Commission
ft-c foot-candle
ft-L foot-lambert
ft-lb foot-pound(s)
ft/sec foot per second
ft-tn foot-ton
fur furlong

G

g gauge; gram
gal gallon(s)
GCA ground control approach
g-cal gram-calorie
GCD greatest common divisor
GCI ground control intercept
gen generator
geo geographic, geography

geol geology, geological, geologist
gpm gallons per minute
gps gallons per second
gr grain; gross
gr wt gross weight
gs ground speed
GSA Geological Society of America

H

h henry (electricity); hour(s)
hcf highest common factor
hdwr hardware
HF high frequency
hl hectoliter
hm hectometer
HMAC Hazardous Materials Advisory Council
HMIS Hazardous Materials Identification System

HMO Health Maintenance Organization
hp high pressure; horsepower
hp-hr horsepower hour
HRB Highway Research Board
HTFMI Heat Transfer and Fluid Mechanics Institute
HW high water
hyp hypothesis

I

IACC International Association of Cereal Chemistry
IAEA International Atomic Energy Agency
IAF International Astronautical Federation
IAMS International Association of Microbiological Societies
IAPA Industrial Accident Prevention Association (Canada)
IAS Institute of Aerospace Sciences
IASS International Association for Shell Structures
IATA International Air Transportation Association
ibp initial boiling point

ICAO International Civil Aviation Organization
ICC Interstate Commerce Commission
ICE Institute of Civil Engineers
ICI International Commission on Illumination
ICLARM International Center for Living Aquatic Resources Management
ICMSF International Commission of Microbiological Specifications for Foods
ICSU International Counsel of Scientific Unions
IDRC International Development Research Center (Canada)
IE industrial engineer

IEA International Energy Agency
IEEE Institute of Electrical and Electronics Engineers
IES Illuminating Engineering Society
IGT Institute of Gas Technology
IGU International Geographical Union
ihp indicated horsepower
IMCO Intergovernmental Maritime Consultative Organization
IMDG International Dangerous Goods Code
IME Institute of Mechanical Engineers
IMMS International Material Management Society
IMO International Maritime Organization
imp gal imperial gallon(s)
IMS International Metallographic Society, Inc.
in inch(es)
INA Institute of Naval Architects
ind industrial
inst instrument
IOC international oceanographic conference
ip intermediate pressure

ips inches per second; intervals per second
IRAC Information Resource and Analysis Center
IRE Institute of Radio Engineers
IRI Industrial Research Institute
IRLG International Regulatory Liaison Group
ISA Instrument Society of America
ISO International Organization for Standardization
ISTM International Society for Testing Materials
ISV international scientific vocabulary
ITU International Telecommunications Union
IUCNNR International Union for Conservation of Nature and Natural Resources
IUFRO International Union of Forest Research Organizations
IUGG International Union of Geodesy and Geophysics
IUPAC International Union of Pure and Applied Chemistry
IWC International Whaling Commission

J

j joule (electricity)
JATO jet assisted take off

JP jet propulsion
junc junction

K

K Kelvin; kilo
kc kilocycle
kcal kilocalorie
kcps kilocycles per second
kg kilogram
kl kiloliter
km kilometer
km² square kilometer

km³ cubic kilometer
kn knot
kt kiloton
kv kilovolt
kva kilovolt-ampere
kw kilowatt
kw-hr kilowatt-hour

L

l   liter; lumen
lab   laboratory
LAGEOS   laser geodetic earth orbiting satellite
LAPI   Labels and Precautionary Information
LASA   large-aperture seismic array
LASER   light amplification by stimulated emission of radiation
lb   pound(s)
lb ap   pound, apothecary's
lb-ft   pound-foot
lb/ft²   pounds per square foot
lb-in   pounds per inch
LC   liquid crystal
LCD   liquid crystal device
lcm   least common multiple
LEO   low earth orbit
LET   linear energy transfer
LF   low frequency
l-hr   lumen hour
LIM   line interface module; liquid injection molding
LIMTV   linear induction motor test vehicle
LIRTS   large infared telescope
LIS   laser isotope separation
lit   liter
LIU   line interface unit

LLC   liquid-liquid chromatography
LMFBR   liquid-metal fast breeder reactor
LMNA   long-range multipurpose naval aircraft
LMWHC   low-molecular weight hydrocarbon
LO   line occupancy
LOAD   laser optoacoustic detection
log   logarithm
LOP   line of position
LOPI   loss of piping integrity
LORAN   long-range navigation
LOSC   Law of the Sea Conference
LOX   liquid oxygen
lp   low pressure
LPG   liquified petroleum gas
lpw   lumens per watt
LREE   light rare-earth element
LRV   lunar roving vehicle
LSD   line sharing device; line signal detector
LSIR   limb scanning infared radiometer
LTTMT   low-temperature thermomechanical treatment
LVDT   linear variable differential transformer
LW   long wave
LWR   light water reactor

M

M   thousand
m   meter; minutes
ma   milliampere
MAA   Mathematical Association of America
MAGLEV   magnetic levitation
MAR   minimum angle of resolution
MASER   microwave amplification by stimulated emission of radiation
math   mathematics
max   maximum
mb   millibar

MC   memory controller
mc   megacycle
MCAA   Mechanical Contractors Association of America
Mcf   million cubic feet
mcps   megacycles per second
MDC   multiple drone control
MEK   methyl ethyl ketone
MEM   minimal essential medium
MEV   million electron volts
MEW   microwave early warning
MF   microfiche

MFMR multifrequency microwave radiometer

MGA multiple gas analyzer

MHD moving head disk

MIKES mass-analyzed ion kenetic energy spectrometry

mks meter-kilogram-second

ml milliliter

MMS multimission modular spacecraft

MODE mid-ocean dynamics experiment

MOL manned orbiting laboratory

MPAI maximum permissible annual intake

MPC maximum permissible concentration

MRAALS marine remote approach and landing system

MRAC meter-reading access circuit

MSBLS microwave scan beam landing system

MSDS material safety data sheet

MSS Manufacturers Standardization Society of the Valve and Fittings Industry; multispectral scanner

MST medium scale technology

MSY maximum sustained yield

MT mean time

MTI moving target indicator

MTS Marine Technology Society

MWE megawatts of electricity

MZ monozygotic

N

N name; neutron; normal; north; number

NACE National Association of Corrosion Engineers

NACM National Association of Chain Manufacturers

NADB National Air Data Branch

NAE National Academy of Engineering

NADW North Atlantic Deep Water

NAL National Accelerator Laboratory

NAM network access machine

NARL Naval Arctic Research Laboratory

NAS National Academy of Sciences

NASA National Aeronautics and Space Administration

NASCO National Academy of Sciences Committee on Oceanography

NASN National Air Surveillance Network

naut nautical

nav naval; navigate; navigation

NavSat navy navigation satellite system

NBC National Building Code; National Building Code of Canada

NBS National Bureau of Standards

NCAES National Center for Analysis of Energy Systems

NCAR National Center for Atmospheric Research

NCB National Coal Board

NCWQ National Commission on Water Quality

NDB nondirectional beacon

NE no effect(s)

NEA negative electron affinity

NEC National Electrical Code; nuclear energy center

NEDS national emission data system

NEG negative

NEI not elsewhere included

NEMA National Electrical Manufacturers Association

NES not elsewhere specified

NESS National Environmental Satellite Service

neurol neurological, neurology

neut neuter

NG no good

NGF nerve growth factor

NIOSH National Institute for Occupational Safety and Health

NM nautical mile

NMAB National Materials Advisory Board

NMC network management center

NMFS National Marine Fisheries Service

No number
NOA National Oceanography Association
NODC National Oceanographic Data Center
NOO United Stated Naval Oceanographic Office
NOP not otherwise provided for
NOS not otherwise specified
NP neuropsychiatric
NPC National Petroleum Council
NPCA National Paint and Coating Association
NPF not provided for
NRAO National Radio Astronomy Observatory
NRC National Research Council; Nuclear Regulatory Commission

NRL Naval Research Laboratory
NS not specified
Ns nimbostratus
NSC National Security Council
NSF National Science Foundation; Nuclear Structure Facility (Great Britain)
NSL National Science Library (Canada)
NSPE National Society of Professional Engineers
NTDPMA National Tool, Die and Precision Machining Association
NTIS National Technical Information Service
NTSB National Transportation Safety Board
NWS National Weather Service

O

O ocean; ohm
OAO orbiting astronomical observatory
OBI omnibearing indicator
obs observation
OCR Office of Coal Research
OCS outer continental shelf
OCZM Office of Coastal Zone Management
OD outside diameter; outside dimension
ODSS ocean dumping surveillance system
ODW organic dry weight
OEDSF onboard experimental data support facility
OES Office of Endangered Species
OFT on flight tests
OLOGS open-loop oxygen-generating system
OMS orbiting maneuvering system
ONR Office of Naval Research

OPEC Organization of Petroleum Exporting Countries
OPO optical parametric oscillator
OPT optical, optics
OPTS Office of Pesticide and Toxic Substances
OR operations research
ORG organic; organized; organization;
ORM other regulated materials
OSA Optical Society of America
OSDR oil slick detection radar
OSF Office of Space Flight
OSHA Occupational Safety and Health Administration
OSR optical solar reflector
OSTP Office of Science and Technology Policy
OTA Office of Technology Assessment
OTEC ocean thermal energy conservation; ocean thermal energy conversion
OTS orbital test satellite
OTV orbital transfer vehicle
oz ounce, ounces

P

PAGEOS   passive geodesic satellite
PAIR   precision approach interfero-
meter radar
PAIT   Program for the Advancement of
Industrial Technology (Canada)
PAR   precision approach radar
PARR   post accident radioactivity remov-
al
PAS   photoacoustic spectroscopy
PBX   plastic bonded explosive
PC   plasma chromatography
PCA   perchloric acid
PDE   partial differential equation;
position-determining equipment
PDS   photodischarge spectroscopy
PE   polyethylene
PEG   polyethylene glycol
PEL   permissible exposure level
PFB   pressurized fluidized bed
PFR   prototype fast reactor
PG   polypropylene glycol
PGS   power generation satellite

PHF   patrol hydrofoil missile
PIXE   proton induced X-ray emission
PLBR   prototype large breeder reactor
PLRS   position, location and reporting
system
PLSS   precision location strike system
POLEX   polar experiment
PPS   plant protection system
PRDPEC   Power Reactor Development
Programme Evaluation Committee
(Canada)
PRS   power relay satellite
PRTM   printing response-time monitor
PSS   public services satellite
PVA   polyvinyl alcohol
PVAC   polyvinyl acetate
PVB   polyvinyl butyral
PVC   polyvinyl chloride
PFV   polyvinyl fluoride
PVS   photovoltaic system
PVT   pressure, volume, temperature
PWR   pressurized, water reactor

Q

Q   quantity; query; question
QAM   quadrature amplitude modulation
QCPSK   quaternary coherent phase-
shift-keyed

QED   quantum electrodynamics
qt   quantity; quart
quad   quadrant
qual   quality
qy   query

R

R   range; roentgen
rad   radical; radio; radius; radix
RAIC   Royal Architectural Association
of Canada
RAR   radio acoustic ranging
RBE   relative biological effectiveness
rc   resistance capacitance

RCRA   Resource Conservation and
Recovery Act
RDF   radio direction finding
RE   rare earth
re   regarding
recip   reciprocal, reciprocity
REE   rare earth element

rept report
rev reverse; revolution
RF radio frequency
RGO Royal Greenwich Observatory (Great Britain)
RH relative humidity
RI refractive index
RIC Rare-Earth Information Center
RIHANS river and harbor aid to navigation system
RIM reaction injection molding
rm ream
RMA Rubber Manufacturers Association
RMI radio magnetic indicator
RMS root mean square
RNA ribonucleic acid

rot rotation
RPH remotely piloted helicopter
RPL rocket propulsion laboratory
RPRV remotely piloted research vehicle
rps revolutions per second
RPV remotely piloted vehicle
RQ reportable quantity
RSA Research Society of America
RSR reactor safety research
RT radio telephone
RTCA Radio Technical Commission for Aeronautics
RTECS Registration of Toxic Effects of Chemical Substances List
RV research vessel
RVR reactor visual range
ry railway

S

S second; section; signal; south; sulfur
SAC Strategic Air Command
SAIT Service d'Analyze de L'information Technologique (Technical Information Analysis Service, Canada)
SAM scanning acoustic microscope
SAMPE Society of Aerospace Material & Process Engineers
SAS Society for Applied Spectroscopy
sat saturate, saturated, saturation
SCAMS scanning microwave spectrometer
SCC satellite communications controller; specialized common carrier
SCD doctor of science
sci science, scientific
scp spherical candlepower
SCUBA self contained underwater breathing apparatus
SD standard deviation
SDC Systems Development Corporation
sec second
sed sediment, sedimentation
SEM scanning electron microscope
sep separate, separated, separation
ser series

SERI Solar Energy Research Institute
SEG Society of Ergonomic Geologists
SES Standards Engineers Society
SESA Society for Experimental Stress Analysis
sg specific gravity
SHA sidereal hour angle
SHF superhigh frequency
shtg shortage
SIAM Society for Industrial and Applied Mathematics
SIC specific inductive capacity; standard industrial classification
SID sudden ionospheric disturbance
sig signal
SIMP satellite information message protocol
sin sine
SIPI Scientists' Institute for Public Information
SIRS satellite infared spectrometer
SL sea level
SLBM submarine launched ballistic missile
SNSO Space Nuclear Systems Office
SOLAS International Conference of Safety of Life at Sea

SOP   standard operating procedure

SOPA   Society for Professional Archeologists

SPIC   Society of the Plastics Industry of Canada

SPIE   Society of Photo-optical Instrumentation Engineers

SPM   solar powered module

SPRDA   Solid Pipeline Research and Development Association (Canada)

SPS   solar power satellite

SPSE   Society of Photographic Scientists and Engineers

SQD   signal quality detector

SR   stimulus-response

SRAM   short range attack missile

SRF   Smithsonian Research Foundation

SSA   Seismological Society of America

SSC   Spectroscopy Society of Canada

SSCV   semisubmersible crane vessel

SSHRC   Social Sciences and Humanities Research Council (Canada)

SSI   ski survey instrument

SSIE   Smithsonian Science Information Exchange

SSME   space shuttle main engine

SSPS   solar-based solar power satellite

SSR   secondary surveillance radar

SSRC   Social Science Research Council of Canada

SSSA   Soil Sciences Society of America

SST   sea surface temperature; supersonic transport

sta   stationary

STAO   Science Teachers Association of Canada

STC   sound transmission class

STDN   space flight tracking and data network

STEM   scanning transmission electron microscope

STP   standard temperature and pressure

STR   submarine thermal reactor

SW   short wave

SWG   standard wire gauge

SWM   shipboard wave meter

sym   symbol, symmetrical

sys   system

T

T   tablespoon; tension; time

t   teaspoon; temperature

TAAC   Technology Assessment Advisory Council

TAB   Technology Assessment Board

tan   tangent

TAS   true air speed

taxon   taxonomy

TBS   talk between ships

tbs   tablespoon

TDN   total digestible nutrients

tech   technical, technically, technician

technol   technological, technology

TEL   tetraethyl lead

tel   telegram; telegraph; telephone

temp   temperature

TH   true heading

theor   theorem

therm   thermal, thermometer

thou   thousand

thp   thrust horsepower

TIS   Technical Information Service

Tl   thallium

TLO   total loss only

TM   technical manual

TMS   The Metallurgical Society

TR   transmit-receive

trans   transmit; transmitter; transaction; transverse

TSCA   Toxic Substances Control Act

TSDF   treatment, storage and disposal facility

TRF   tuned radio frequency

trig   trigonometry

ts   tensile strength

TU   transmission unit

TV   television; terminal velocity

typ   typographical

U

U   unit
UDC   universal decimal classification
UHF   ultra high frequency
UL   Underwriter's Laboratory
UNEP   United Nations Environment Program
UNESCO   United Nations Educational, Scientific and Cultural Organization
UNIS   underwater television and inspection system
USDA   United States Department of Agriculture
UTS   underwater telephone system
UV   ultra violet

V

V   vector; velocity; volume; voltage
vac   vacuum
VCO   voltage-controlled oscillator
VCR   variable compression ratio
VD   vapor density
vert   vertical
VF   video frequency
VHF   very high frequency
VI   volume indicator
vis   visibility, visual
VLF   very low frequency
VLR   very long range
VOR   very high frequency omni range
VP   variable pitch
VT   vacuum tube
Vt   video terminal
VTOL   vertical take off and landing
VU   volume unit

W

WAITRO   World Association of Industrial and Technological Research Organizations (Canada)
WL   wavelength
wmk   watermark
WMO   World Meteorological Organization
wpc   watts per candle
WRNE   Whiteshell Nuclear Research Establishment (Canada)
WRSIC   Water Resources Scientific Information Center
WT   watertight; weight; wireless telegraphy

X

X   experimental
XPS   X-ray photoelectron spectroscopy
XTC   external transmit clock

Y

y   yard; year
YBP   years before present

yr   year

Z

Z   zero; zone
Zoochem   zoochemistry

zoogeog   zoogeography
zool   zoological; zoology

6

TITLES, DEGREES, APPELLATIONS

(Awards; Professional Designations and Associations; Fraternities; The Military)

A

A   associate in arts
AAA   Anti-Aircraft Artillery
AAC   Army Air Corps
aag   assistant adjutant general
AAF   Army Air Forces
AAONMS   Ancient Arabic Order of the Nobles of the Mystic Shrine
AASR   Ancient Accepted Scottish Rite (Masonic)
AB   Bachelor of Arts
AC   Air Corps
actg   acting
adc   aide-de-camp
adj   adjutant; adjunct
adj gen   adjutant general
adm   admiral
AE   agricultural engineer
AE and P   Ambassador Extraordinary and Plenipotentiary
AEF   American Expeditionary Forces
AFB   Air Force Base
AFD   doctor of fine arts
AF and AM   Ancient Free and Accepted Masons
AFTRA   American Federation TV and Radio Artists

AIA   American Institute of Architects
Am Inst EE   American Institute of Electrical Engineers
Am Soc CE   American Society of Civil Engineers
Am Soc ME   American Society of Mechanical Engineers
ANA   Associate National Academician
ANTA   American National Theatre and Academy
antiq   antiquarian
AOH   Ancient Order of Hibernians
apptd   appointed
aqm   assistant quartermaster
Arts D   doctor of arts
AS   Air Service
ASCAP   American Society of Composers, Authors and Publishers
ASF   Air Service Force
asso   associate; associated
asst   assistant
ATSC   Air Technical Service Command
Atty   attorney
AUS   Army of the United States
Aux   Auxiliary

B

B   bachelor
BA   bachelor of arts
BAAS   British Association for the Advancement of Science
BAgr   bachelor of agriculture
BArch   bachelor of architecture
BAS   bachelor of agricultural science
batn   battalion
batt   battalion
BBA   bachelor of business administration
BASc   bachelor of applied science
BCE   bachelor of civil engineering
BChir   bachelor of surgery
BCL   bachelor of civil law
BCS   bachelor of commercial science
BD   bachelor of divinity
BDI   bachelor of didactics
BE   bachelor of education
BEE   bachelor of electrical engineering
BEF   British Expeditionary Force
BFA   bachelor of fine arts

BJ   bachelor of journalism
BL   bachelor of letters
BLS   bachelor of library science
Bn   battalion
BO   bachelor of oratory
BP   bachelor of painting
BPE   bachelor of physical education
BPOE   Benevolent and Protective Order of Elks
BPd   bachelor of pedagogy
BRE   bachelor of religious education
brig   brigade; brigadier
brig gen   brigadier general
Bro   Brother
BS   bachelor of science
BS in Ry ME   bachelor in railway mechanical engineering
BSA   bachelor of agricultural science
BSD   bachelor of didactic science
BST   bachelor of sacred theology
BTh   bachelor of theology

C

CAC   Coast Artillery Corps
cpt   captain
cav   cavalry
CBI   China–Burma–India theater of operations
CE   civil engineer (degree); Corps of Engineers
CEF   Canadian Expeditionary Forces
ChD   doctor of chemistry
ChemE   chemical engineer
Chirurg   Chirurgical
chmn   chairman
CIA   Central Intelligence Agency
CIC   Counter Intelligence Corps
CLU   Certified Life Underwriter
CM   master in surgery
COF   Catholic Order of Foresters
col   colonel
comd   commanded
comdg   commanding

comdr   commander
comdt   commandant
commd   commissioned
commr   commissioner
Com Sub   Commissary of Subsistence
condr   conductor
cons   consultant; consulting
corr   correspondent
CPA   Certified Public Accountant
CPCU   Chartered Property and Casualty Underwriter
CPH   Certificate of Public Health
cpl   corporal
CS Army   Confederate State Army
CSB   bachelor of Christian Science
CSD   doctor of Christian Science
CSN   Confederate States Navy
CT   candidate in theology
CWS   Chemical Warfare Service

D

D   doctor
D Agr   doctor of agriculture
DAR   Daughters of the American Revolution
DAV   Disabled American Veterans
DCL   doctor of civil law
DCS   doctor of commercial science
DD   doctor of divinity
DDS   doctor of dental surgery
Def   defense
del   delegate
Dem   Democratic
DEng   doctor of engineering
dep   deputy
DFC   Distinguished Flying Cross
DHL   doctor of Hebrew literature
dir   director
DLitt   doctor of literature

DMD   doctor of medical dentistry
DMS   doctor of medical science
DO   doctor of osteopathy
DPA   Defense Production Administration
DPH   diploma in public health; doctor of public health; doctor of public hygiene
Dr   doctor
DR   Daughters of the Revolution
DRE   doctor of religious education
DSc   doctor of science
DSC   Distinguished Service Cross
DSM   Distinguished Service Medal
DST   doctor of sacred theology
DTM   doctor of tropical medicine
DVN   doctor of veterinary medicine
DVS   doctor of veterinary surgery

E

E AND P   Extraordinary and Plenipotentiary
eccles   ecclesiastical
EdB   bachelor of education
EdD   doctor of education
EdM   master of education
EE   electrical engineer
EE and MP   Envoy Extraordinary and Minister Plenipotentiary
EM   engineer of mines
engr   engineer
ESMWTP   Engineering, Science and Management War Training Program
ETO   European Theater of Operations
Evang   Evangelical

F

F   Fellow
FA   Field Artillery
FACP   Fellow American College of Physicians
FACS   Fellow American College of Surgeons

FE   forest engineer
frat   fraternity
FRCP   Fellow Royal College of Physicians (England)
FRCS   Fellow Royal College of Surgeons (England)

G

G-1 (or other number), Division of General Staff
GAR Grand Army of the Republic
GD graduate in divinity

gen general
GHQ General Headquarters
gov governor

H

HG Home Guard
HHD doctor of humanities
HM master of humanities

hon honorary; honorable
Ho of Reps House of Representatives
HR House of Representatives

I

IEEE Institute of Electrical and Electronics Engineers
Ind Independent
inf infantry
instr instructor
IOBB Independent Order of B'nai B'rith

IOGT Independent Order of Good Templars
IOOF Independent Order of Odd Fellows
IRE Institute of Radio Engineers

J

JB jurum baccalaureus
JCB juris canonici bachelor
JCL jurus canonici lector
JD doctor of jurisprudence

jr junior
JSD doctor of juristic science
JUD juris utriusque doctor; doctor of both (canon and civil) laws

K

KC Knight of Columbus
KCCH Knight Commander of Court of Honor

KP Knight of Pythias

L

lectr   lecturer
LHD   doctor of letters of humanity
lieut   lieutenant
Lit Hum   Literae Humanores (classics, Oxford University, England)
LittB   bachelor of letters
LittD   doctor of letters
LLB   bachelor of laws
LLD   doctor of laws

LLM   master of laws
LOM   Loyal Order of Moose
LRCP   Licentiate Royal College of Physicians
LRCS   Licentiate Royal College of Surgeons
LS   Library Science
LSA   Licentiate Society of Apothecaries
lt   lieutenant

M

MA   master of arts
MAgr   master of agriculture
maj   major
MArch   master in architecture
MASc   master of applied science
MB   bachelor of medicine
MBA   master of business administration
MC   Medical Corps
MCS   master of commercial science
MD   doctor of medicine
MDi   master of didactics
MDip   master of diplomacy
MDV   doctor of veterinary medicine
ME   mechanical engineer
MEd   master of education
Med ORC   Medical Officers' Reserve Corps
Med RC   Medical Reserve Corps
MEE   master of electrical engineering
MetE   metallurgical engineer
MF   master of forestry
MFA   master of fine arts
MHA   master of hospital administration
MI   Military Intelligence
ML   master of laws
MLitt   master of literature

Mlle   Mademoiselle (Miss)
MLS   master of library science
Mme   Madame
MME   master of mechanical engineering
MP   Member of Parliament
MPd   master of pedagogy
MPE   master of physical education
MPL   master of patent law
MRCP   Member Royal College of Physicians
MRCS   Member Royal College of Surgeons
MRE   master of religious education
MS   master of science
MSc   master of science
MSF   master of science of forestry
MST   master of sacred theology
MSW   master of social work
MTOUSA   Mediterranean Theater of Operations, U.S. Army
MusB   bachelor of music
MusD   (or Mus Doc), doctor of music
MusM   master of music
MVM   Massachusetts Volunteer Militia
MWA   Modern Woodmen of America

N

NA   National Academician; National Army

NAACP   National Association for the Advancement of Colored People

NAD   National Academy of Design

NAM   National Association of Manufacturers

NATOUSA   North African Theater of Operations, U.S. Army

NEA   National Education Association

NG   National Guard

NGSNY   National Guard State of New York

NPhD   Doctor of Natural Philosophy

O

OB   bachelor of oratory

OES   Order of the Eastern Star

OQMG   Office of Quartermaster General

ORC   Officers' Reserve Corps

OSB   Order of Saint Benedict

OTC   Officers' Training Camp

OTS   Officers' Training School

OUAM   Order of United American Mechanics

P

PdB   bachelor of pedagogy

PdD   doctor of pedagogy

PdM   master of pedagogy

PeB   bachelor of pediatrics

PEN   Poets, Playwrights, Editors, Essayists and Novelists (International Association)

pfc   private first class

PharmD   doctor of pharmacy

PharmM   master of pharmacy

PhB   bachelor of philosophy

PhD   doctor of philosophy

PhG   graduate in pharmacy

Phys and Surg   Physicians and Surgeons (college at Columbia University)

PM   prime minister

pres   president

prof   professor

propr   proprietor

pros atty   prosecuting attorney

PTA   Parent-Teacher Association

PTO   Pacific Theatre of Operations

pvt   private

Py B   bachelor of pedagogy

Q

qm   quartermaster

QMC   Quartermaster Corps

qm gen   quartermaster general

QMORC   Quartermaster Officers' Reserve Corps

R

RAF Royal Air Force
RAM Royal Arch Mason
RC Reserve Corps
RCAF Royal Canadian Air Force
Ref Reformed
Regt Regiment
Rep Republican
rep representative
ret retired

Rev Reverend, Review
RN registered nurse
ROSC Reserve Officers' Sanitary Corps
ROTC Reserve Officers' Training Corps
RPD rerum politicarum doctor (doctor political science)
RTC Reserve Training Corps

S

SAC Strategic Air Command
SAR Sons of the American Revolution
SATC Students' Army Training Corps
SB bachelor of science
SCAP Supreme Command Allies Pacific
ScD (or DSc), doctor of science
SCD doctor of commercial science
SCV Sons of Confederate Veterans
sec secretary
Sem Seminary
sgt sergeant
SHAEF Supreme Headquarters, Allied Expeditionary Forces
SHAPE Supreme Headquarters Allied Powers in Europe

SJ Society of Jesus (Jesuit)
SJD doctor juristic science
SM master of science
soc society
S of V Sons of Veterans
SRC Signal Reserve Corps
sr senior
SR Sons of the Revolution
St Saint
STB bachelor of sacred theology
STD doctor of sacred theology
STL licentiate in sacred theology; lector of sacred theology
supr supervisor
supt superintendent

T

TAPPI Technical Association Pulp and Paper Industry
Tchrs Teachers
ThD doctor of theology

ThM master of theology
TPA Travelers Protective Association
treas treasurer

U

UB United Brethren in Christ
UCV United Confederate Veterans
UDC United Daughters of the Confederacy
USAAF United States Army Air Force
USAC United States Air Corps
USAF United States Air Force
USCG United States Coast Guard
USCT United States Colored Troops
USMC United States Marine Corps

USMHS United States Marine Hospital Service
USN United States Navy
USNA United States National Army
USNG United States National Guard
USNRF United States Naval Reserve Force
USR United States Reserve
USV United States Volunteers

V

VA Veterans Administration
vet veteran; veterinary
VFW Veterans of Foreign Wars

vice pres vice president
vol volunteer

W

WAC Women's Army Corps
WAVES Women's Reserve, United States Naval Reserve

WCTU Women's Christian Temperance Union
WPB War Production Board

Y

YMCA Young Men's Christian Association
YMHA Young Men's Hebrew Association
YM and YWHA Young Men's and

Young Women's Hebrew Association
YWCA Young Women's Christian Association
YWHA Young Women's Hebrew Association

7

U.S. STATES AND PROTECTORATES; CANADIAN PROVINCES AND TERRITORIES

a. U.S. STATES AND PROTECTORATES

AK	Alaska		MT	Montana
AL	Alabama		NC	North Carolina
AR	Arkansas		ND	North Dakota
AZ	Arizona		NE	Nebraska
CA	California		NH	New Hampshire
CO	Colorado		NJ	New Jersey
CT	Connecticut		NM	New Mexico
DC	District of Columbia		NV	Nevada
DE	Delaware		NY	New York
FL	Florida		OH	Ohio
GA	Georgia		OK	Oklahoma
GU	Guam		OR	Oregon
HI	Hawaii		PA	Pennsylvania
IA	Iowa		PR	Puerto Rico
ID	Idaho		RI	Rhode Island
IL	Illinois		SC	South Carolina
IN	Indiana		SD	South Dakota
KS	Kansas		TN	Tennessee
KY	Kentucky		TX	Texas
LA	Louisiana		UT	Utah
MA	Maine		VA	Virginia
MD	Maryland		VI	Virgin Islands
ME	Maine		VT	Vermont
MI	Michigan		WA	Washington
MN	Minnesota		WI	Wisconsin
MO	Missouri		WV	West Virginia
MS	Mississippi		WY	Wyoming

b. U.S. STATES AND PROTECTORATES REVERSE DICTIONARY

Alabama	AL		Indiana	IN
Alaska	AK		Iowa	IA
Arizona	AZ		Kansas	KS
Arkansas	AR		Kentucky	KY
California	CA		Louisiana	LA
Colorado	CO		Maine	ME
Connecticut	CT		Maryland	MD
Delaware	DE		Massachusetts	MA
District of Columbia	DC		Michigan	MI
Florida	FL		Minnesota	MN
Georgia	GA		Mississippi	MS
Guam	GU		Missouri	MO
Hawaii	HI		Montana	MT
Idaho	ID		Nebraska	NE
Illinois	IL		Nevada	NV

New Hampshire	**NH**		South Dakota	**SD**
New Mexico	**NM**		Tennessee	**TN**
New York	**NY**		Texas	**TX**
North Carolina	**NC**		Utah	**UT**
North Dakota	**ND**		Vermont	**VT**
Ohio	**OH**		Virgin Islands	**VI**
Oklahoma	**OK**		Virginia	**VA**
Oregon	**OR**		Washington	**WA**
Pennsylvania	**PA**		West Virginia	**WV**
Puerto Rico	**PR**		Wisconsin	**WI**
Rhode Island	**RI**		Wyoming	**WY**
South Carolina	**SC**			

c. CANADIAN PROVINCES AND TERRITORIES

Alta	Alberta		**NWT**	Northwest Territories
BC	British Columbia		**Ont**	Ontario
Lab	Labrador		**PEI**	Prince Edward Island
Man	Manitoba		**Que**	Quebec
NB	New Brunswick		**Sask**	Saskatchewan
Nfld	Newfoundland		**Yuk**	Yukon Territories
NS	Nova Scotia			

d. CANADIAN PROVINCES AND TERRITORIES
(two-letter abbreviations)

Although there is no standard, the two-letter abbreviations given here are coming into common use in the automated office.

AB	Alberta		**NT**	Northwest Territories
BC	British Columbia		**ON**	Ontario
LB	Labrador		**PE**	Prince Edward Island
MB	Manitoba		**PQ**	Quebec
NB	New Brunswick		**SK**	Saskatchewan
NF	Newfoundland		**YT**	Yukon Territory
NS	Nova Scotia			

e. CANADIAN PROVINCES AND TERRITORIES
REVERSE DICTIONARY

Alberta	**AB**		Nova Scotia	**NS**
British Columbia	**BC**		Ontario	**ON**
Labrador	**LB**		Prince Edward Island	**PE**
Manitoba	**MB**		Quebec	**PQ**
New Brunswick	**NB**		Saskatchewan	**SK**
Newfoundland	**NF**		Yukon Territory	**YT**
Northwest Territories	**NT**			

8
STREETS AND ADDRESSES

A

Aly	alley	**Arc**	arcade
Anx	annex	**Ave**	avenue
Arprt	airport		

B

Bch	beach	**Brg**	bridge
Blf	bluff	**Brk**	brook
Blvd	boulevard	**Byp**	bypass
Bnd	bend	**Byu**	bayou
Br	branch		

C

Chr	church	**Crk**	creek
Cir	circle	**Ct**	court
Clfs	cliffs	**Ctl**	central
Clg	college	**Ctr**	center
Cor	corner	**Cts**	courts
Cors	corners	**Cv**	cove
Cp	camp	**Cwsy**	causeway
Cpe	cape	**Cy**	city
Cres	crescent	**Cyn**	canyon

D

Div	divide	**Dpo**	depo
Dl	dale	**Dr**	drive
Dm	dam		

E

E	east	**Expy**	expressway
Est	estates	**Ext**	extension

F

Fld	field	**Frks**	forks
Flds	fields	**Frms**	farms
Fls	falls	**Frst**	forest
Flt	flat	**Fry**	ferry
Flts	flats	**Ft**	fort
Frd	ford	**Ftn**	fountain
Frg	forge	**Furn**	furnace
Frk	fork	**Fwy**	freeway

G

Gdns	gardens	**Grn**	green
Gln	glen	**Grnd**	grand
Gr	great	**Grv**	grove
Grd	ground	**Gtwy**	gateway

H

Hbr	harbor	**Hosp**	hospital
Hglds	highlands	**Hse**	house
Hl	hill	**Hts**	heights
Hls	hills	**Hvn**	haven
Holw	hollow	**Hwy**	highway

I

Inlt	inlet	**Is**	island(s); isle
Inst	institute		

J

Jct	junction

K

Knls	knolls	**Ky**	key

L

Lcks	locks	**Lndg**	landing
Ldg	lodge	**Ln**	lane
Lk	lake	**Ltl**	little
Lks	lakes	**Lwr**	lower

M

Mdws	meadows	**Mls**	mills
Mdl	middle	**Mnr**	manor
Mem	memorial	**Mns**	mines
Ml	mill	**Msn**	mission
Mle	mile	**Mt**	mount

N

N	north	**Nw**	new
Nat	national		

O

Orch   orchard

P

Pk	park	Plz	plaza
Pky	parkway	Pnes	pines
Pl	place	Pr	prairie
Plms	palms	Prt	port
Pln	plain	Pt	point
Plns	plains		

R

R	rural	Rk	rock
Rd	road	Rnch	ranch
Rdg	ridge	Rnchs	ranches
Resrt	resort	Rpds	rapids
Riv	river	RR	rural route

S

S	south	Sn	San; Santa; Santo
Sch	school	Spg	spring
Shl	shoal	Spgs	springs
Shls	shoals	Sq	square
Shr	shore	Ste	Saint; Sainte; state; street
Shrs	shores	Sta	station
Smnry	seminary	Strm	stream
Smt	summit		

T

Tce	terrace	Tunl	tunnel
Ter	terrace	Tvrn	tavern
Term	terminal	Twn	town
Tpke	turnpike	Twr	tower
Trl	trail		

U

Univ	university		**Upr**	upper

V

Vg	village		**Vl**	ville
Via	viaduct		**Vly**	valley
Vis	vista		**Vw**	view

W

W	west		**Wls**	wells
Wks	works			

X

Xing	crossing

Y

Yd	yard		**Yds**	yards

9
CHEMICAL ELEMENTS

a. CHEMICAL ELEMENTS

Ac	Actinium	Mn	Manganese
Ag	Silver	Mo	Molybdenum
Al	Aluminum	N	Nitrogen
Am	Americium	Na	Sodium
As	Arsenic	Nb	Niobium
At	Astatine	Nd	Neodymium
Au	Gold	Ne	Neon
B	Boron	Ni	Nickle
Ba	Barium	No	Nobelium
Be	Beryllium	Np	Neptunium
Bi	Bismuth	O	Oxygen
Bk	Berkelium	Os	Osmium
Br	Bromine	P	Phosphorus
C	Carbon	Pa	Protatinium
Ca	Calcium	Pb	Lead
Cd	Cadmium	Pd	Palladium
Ce	Cerium	Pm	Promethium
Cf	Californium	Po	Polonium
Cl	Chlorine	Pr	Praseodymium
Cm	Curium	Pt	Platinum
Co	Cobalt	Pu	Plutonium
Cr	Chromium	Ra	Radium
Cs	Cesium	Rb	Rubidium
Cu	Copper	Re	Rhenium
Dy	Dysprosium	Rh	Rhodium
Er	Erbium	Rn	Radon
Es	Einsteinium	Ru	Ruthenium
Eu	Europium	S	Sulfur
F	Florine	Sb	Antimony
Fe	Iron	Sc	Scandium
Fm	Fermium	Se	Selenium
Fr	Francium	Si	Silicon
Ga	Gallium	Sm	Samarium
Gd	Gadolinium	Sn	Tin
Ge	Germanium	Sr	Strontium
H	Hydrogen	Ta	Tantalum
He	Helium	Tb	Terbium
Hf	Hafnium	Tc	Technetium
Hg	Mercury	Te	Tellurium
Ho	Holmium	Th	Thorium
I	Iodine	Ti	Titanium
In	Indium	Tl	Thallium
Ir	Iridium	Tm	Thulium
K	Potassium	U	Uranium
Kr	Krypton	V	Vanadium
La	Lanthanum	W	Tungsten
Li	Lithium	Xe	Xenon
Lr	Laurencium	Y	Yttrium
Lu	Lutetium	Yb	Ytterbium
Lw	Lawrencium	Zn	Zinc
Md	Mendelevium	Zr	Zirconium
Mg	Magnesium		

b. CHEMICAL ELEMENTS REVERSE DICTIONARY WITH ATOMIC NUMBERS

ELEMENT	ABBRE-VIATION	ATOMIC NUMBER	ELEMENT	ABBRE-VIATION	ATOMIC NUMBER
Actinium	Ac	89	Lanthanum	La	57
Aluminum	Al	13	Lawrencium	Lr (Lw)	103
Americium	Am	95	Lead	Pb	82
Antimony	Sb	51	Lithium	Li	3
Arsenic	As	33	Lutetium	Lu	71
Astatine	At	85	Magnesium	Mg	12
Barium	Ba	56	Maganese	Mn	25
Berkelium	Bk	97	Mendelevium	Md	101
Beryllium	Be	4	Mercury	Hg	80
Bismuth	Bi	83	Molybdenum	Mo	42
Boron	B	5	Neodymium	Nd	60
Bromine	Br	35	Neon	Ne	10
Cadmium	Cd	48	Neptunium	Np	93
Calcium	Ca	20	Nickle	Ni	28
Californium	Cf	98	Niobium	Nb	41
Carbon	C	6	Nitrogen	N	7
Cerium	Ce	58	Nobelium	No	102
Cesium	Cs	55	Osmium	Os	76
Chlorine	Cl	17	Oxygen	O	8
Chromium	Cr	24	Palladium	Pd	46
Cobalt	Co	27	Phosphorus	P	15
Copper	Cu	29	Platinum	Pt	78
Curium	Cm	96	Plutonium	Pu	94
Dysprosium	Dy	66	Polonium	Po	84
Einsteinium	Es	99	Potassium	K	19
Erbium	Er	68	Praseodymium	Pr	59
Europium	Eu	63	Promethium	Pm	61
Fermium	Fm	100	Protatinium	Pa	91
Florine	F	9	Radium	Ra	88
Francium	Fr	87	Radon	Rn	86
Gadolinium	Gd	64	Rhenium	Re	75
Gallium	Ga	31	Rhodium	Rh	45
Germanium	Ge	32	Rubidium	Rb	37
Gold	Au	79	Ruthenium	Ru	44
Hafnium	Hf	72	Samarium	Sm	62
Helium	He	2	Scandium	Sc	21
Holmium	Ho	67	Selenium	Se	34
Hydrogen	H	1	Silicon	Si	14
Indium	In	49	Silver	Ag	47
Iodine	I	53	Sodium	Na	11
Iridium	Ir	77	Strontium	Sr	38
Iron	Fe	26	Sulfur	S	16
Krypton	Kr	36	Tantalum	Ta	73

ELEMENT	ABBRE-VIATION	ATOMIC NUMBER	ELEMENT	ABBRE-VIATION	ATOMIC NUMBER
Technetium	Tc	43	**Tungsten**	W	74
Tellurium	Te	52	**Uranium**	U	92
Terbium	Tb	65	**Vanadium**	V	23
Thallium	Tl	81	**Xenon**	Xe	54
Thorium	Th	90	**Ytterbium**	Yb	70
Thulium	Tm	69	**Yttrium·**	Y	39
Tin	Sn	50	**Zinc**	Zn	30
Titanium	Ti	22	**Zirconium**	Zr	40

10
SPECIAL SYMBOLS

†	dagger, death or deceased
§	section
§§	sections
¶	paragraph
¶¶	paragraphs
©	copyright
™	trademark
sm	service mark
®	registered
@	at
$	dollar sign
#	number, when used before a figure
#	pounds, when used after a figure
%	percent
*	asterisk
&	ampersand ("and")
<	less than
>	greater than
=	equals
+	plus, positive
−	minus, negative

11
SUGGESTED READING AND REFERENCE GUIDES

(Data Processing; Data Processing, Computer Technology; Computer Systems and Programming; Computer Security; Database; Networks; Microcomputers; Word Processing; Secretarial/ Office Procedures; Office Automation; Legal Reference Books; Business Reference Books; Medical Dictionaries and Reference Books; Industrial and Scientific References).

The abbreviations and acronyms in this work were compiled from well over 100 sources. Following is a selected list of reference in the subject areas covered, as well as suggestions for further reading that may be of interest.

a. DATA PROCESSING AND COMPUTER DICTIONARIES

Chandor, Anthony. *The Penguin Dictionary of Computers.* New York: Penguin Books, 1982.

Darcy, Laura, and Boston, Louise. *Webster's New World Dictionary of Computer Terms.* New York: Simon & Schuster, 1983.

Hordeski, Michael. *Illustrated Dictionary of Microcomputer Terminology.* Blue Ridge Summit, PA: TAB Books, 1980.

Illustrated Computer Dictionary. New York: Simon & Schuster, 1983.

Sippl, Charles J. *Computer Dictionary and Handbook.* New York: Bobbs-Merrill, 1967.

——————————. *Microcomputer Dictionary*, 2nd edition. Indianapolis: Howard W. Sams & Co., 1981.

b. DATA PROCESSING, COMPUTER TECHNOLOGY, COMPUTER SYSTEMS AND PROGRAMMING

Douglas, Jack L., and Zupko, Bill. *More About Modems.* Huntsville, AL: United Data Systems, 1983.

Grauer, Robert T. *The IBM Cobol Environment.* Englewood Cliffs, NJ: Prentice Hall, 1984.

Hunter, Robin. *The Design and Construction of Compilers.* New York: John Wiley & Sons, 1981.

Kapp, Don, and Leben, Joseph F. *IMS Programming Techniques.* New York: Van Nostrand Reinhold, 1978.

Madnick, Stuart E., and Donovan, John J. *Operating Systems.* New York: McGraw-Hill, 1974.

Parkin, Andrew. *Systems Analysis.* Cambridge, MA: Winthrop Publishers, 1980.

Ralston, Anthony, and Reilly, Edwin D., Jr. *Encyclopedia of Computer Science and Engineering.* New York: Van Nostrand Reinhold, 1983.

Stabley, Don H. *Assembler Language for Application Programming.* New York: Petrocelli Books, 1982.

c. COMPUTER SECURITY

Cooper, James Arlin. *Computer-Security Technology.* Lexington, MA: D. C. Heath & Co., 1984.

Hoffman, Lance J. *Security and Privacy in Computer Systems.* Los Angeles: Melville Publishing, 1973.

d. DATABASE

Date, C. J. *Database: A Primer.* Reading, MA: Addison-Wesley, 1983.

Kruglinski, David. *Database Management Systems.* Berkeley, CA: Osborne/McGraw-Hill, 1983.

e. NETWORKS

Derfler, Frank, and Stallings, William. *A Manager's Guide to Local Networks.* Englewood Cliffs, NJ: Prentice Hall, 1983.

f. MICROCOMPUTERS

Christie, Linda Gail, and Currey, Jess W., Jr. *The ABCs of Microcomputers: A Computer Literacy Primer.* Englewood Cliffs, NJ: Prentice Hall, 1983.

g. WORD PROCESSING

Clippinger, Dorinda A. *Word Processing Input.* Englewood Cliffs, NJ: Prentice-Hall, 1982.

Flores, Ivan. *Word Processing Handbook.* New York: Van Nostrand Reinhold, 1983.

Greenia, Mark W. *Professional Word Processing in Business and Legal Environments.* Englewood Cliffs, NJ: Reston Publishing/Prentice-Hall, 1985.

Sikonowiz, Walter. *Word Processing and Business Graphics.* Englewood Cliffs, NJ: Micro Text Publications/Prentice-Hall, 1982.

h. SECRETARIAL/OFFICE PROCEDURES

Hutchinson, Lois. *Standard Handbook for Secretaries.* New York: McGraw-Hill, 1979.

Jennings, Lucy Mae. *Secretarial and Administrative Procedures.* Englewood Cliffs, NJ: Prentice-Hall, 1982.

Webster's New World Secretarial Handbook. New York: Simon & Schuster, 1981.

i. OFFICE AUTOMATION

Aschner, Katherine. *The Word Processing Handbook.* North Vancouver, B.C.: International Self-Counsel Press, 1983.

Green, James H. *Automating Your Office.* New York: McGraw-Hill, 1984.

Katzan, Harry Jr. *Office Automation: A Manager's Guide.* New York: Amacon Book Division of American Management Association, 1982.

j. LEGAL REFERENCE BOOKS

Black, Henry C. *Black's Law Dictionary*, 6th edition. St. Paul, MN: West Publishing, 1985.

Giffs, Steven H. *Law Dictionary.* Woodbury, NY: Barron's Educational Series, 1975.

k. BUSINESS REFERENCE BOOKS

Oran, Daniel, and Shafritz, Jay M. *The MBAs Dictionary.* Reston, VA: Reston Publishing Co., 1983.

l. MEDICAL DICTIONARIES AND REFERENCE BOOKS

Blakiston's Pocket Medical Dictionary. New York: McGraw-Hill, 1979.

Dox, Ida et al. *Melloni's Illustrated Medical Dictionary*. Baltimore, MD: Williams and Wickins Co., 1979.

Kruzas, Anthony T. *Encyclopedia of Medical Organizations and Agencies*. Detroit: Gale Research Co., 1983.

Saunders, W. B. *Dorland's Illustrated Medical Dictionary*. Philadelphia: Holt Rinehart and Winston, 1981.

m. INDUSTRIAL AND SCIENTIFIC REFERENCES

Douglas-Young, John. *Illustrated Encyclopedic Dictionary of Electronics*. West Nyack, NY: Parker Publishing Co., 1981.

Parker, Sybil P. *McGraw-Hill Encyclopedia of Engineering*. New York: McGraw-Hill, 1983.

CANADIAN

ORDER FORM

10/85

SELF-COUNSEL SERIES

NATIONAL TITLES:

	Title	Price
_____	Aids to Independence	11.95
_____	Assertiveness for Managers	8.95
_____	Basic Accounting	5.95
_____	Be a Better Manager	7.95
_____	Better Book for Getting Hired	9.95
_____	Business Guide to Effective Speaking	6.95
_____	Business Guide to Telephone Systems	7.95
_____	Business Writing Workbook	9.95
_____	Buying (and Selling) a Small Business	6.95
_____	Changing Your Name in Canada	3.50
_____	Civil Rights	8.95
_____	Collection Techniques for the Small Business	4.95
_____	Complete Guide to Being Your Own Home Contractor	19.95
_____	Credit, Debt, and Bankruptcy	5.95
_____	Criminal Procedure in Canada	12.95
_____	Design Your Own Logo	9.95
_____	Drinking and Driving	4.50
_____	Editing Your Newsletter	14.95
_____	Exporting	12.50
_____	Family Ties That Bind	7.95
_____	Federal Incorporation and Business Guide	12.95
_____	Financial Control for the Small Business	5.95
_____	Financial Freedom on $5 A Day	6.95
_____	For Sale By Owner	4.95
_____	Franchising in Canada	6.50
_____	Fundraising	5.50
_____	Getting Elected	
_____	Getting Sales	14.95
_____	Getting Started	11.95
_____	How to Advertise	7.95
_____	How You Too Can Make a Million . . . In the Mail Order Business	8.95
_____	Immigrating to Canada	14.95
_____	Immigrating to the U.S.A.	14.95
_____	Importing	21.95
_____	Insuring Business Risks	3.50
_____	Keyboarding for Kids	7.95
_____	Landlording in Canada	12.95
_____	Learn to Type Fast	6.50
_____	Life Insurance for Canadians	3.50
_____	Managing Your Office Records and Files	14.95
_____	Managing Stress	7.95
_____	Media Law Handbook	6.50
_____	Medical Law Handbook	6.95
_____	Mike Grenby's Money Book	5.50
_____	Mike Grenby's Tax Tips	
_____	Mortgage and Foreclosure Handbook	6.95
_____	Musician's Handbook	7.95
_____	Parents' Guide to Day Care	5.95
_____	Practical Guide to Financial Management	5.95
_____	Ready-to-Use Business Forms	9.95
_____	Resort Condos	4.50
_____	Retirement Guide for Canadians	9.95
_____	Start and Run a Profitable Beauty Salon	14.95
_____	Start and Run a Profitable Consulting Business	12.95
_____	Start and Run a Profitable Craft Business	10.95
_____	Start and Run a Profitable Home Typing Business	9.95
_____	Start and Run a Profitable Restaurant	10.95
_____	Start and Run a Profitable Retail Business	11.95
_____	Start and Run a Video Store	10.95
_____	Starting a Successful Business in Canada	12.95
_____	Tax Law Handbook	12.95
_____	Taxpayer Alert!	4.95
_____	Tax Shelters	6.95
_____	Trusts and Trust Companies	3.95
_____	Upper Left-Hand Corner	10.95
_____	Using the Access to Information Act	5.95
_____	Word Processing	8.95
_____	Working Couples	5.50
_____	Write Right!	(Cloth) 5.95 / (Paper) 5.50

PROVINCIAL TITLES:
Please indicate which provincial edition is required.

Consumer Book
☐B.C. 7.95   ☐Ontario 6.95

Divorce Guide
☐B.C. 12.95 ☐Alberta 9.95 ☐Ontario ☐Man./Sask.

Employee/Employer Rights
☐B.C. 6.95 ☐Alberta 6.95 ☐Ontario 6.95

Fight That Ticket
☐B.C. 5.95 ☐Ontario 3.95

Incorporation Guide
☐B.C. 14.95 ☐Alberta 14.95 ☐Ontario 14.95 ☐Man./Sask. 12.95

Landlord/Tenant Rights
☐B.C.   ☐Alberta 5.50 ☐Ontario 6.95

Marriage & Family Law
☐B.C. 7.95 ☐Alberta 5.95 ☐Ontario 7.95

Probate Guide
☐B.C. 12.95 ☐Alberta 9.95 ☐Ontario 9.95

Real Estate Guide
☐B.C. 7.95 ☐Alberta 7.95 ☐Ontario 7.95

Small Claims Court Guide
☐B.C. 6.95 ☐Alberta 7.50 ☐Ontario 5.95

Wills
☐B.C. 5.95 ☐Alberta 5.95 ☐Ontario 5.50

Wills/Probate Procedure
☐Man./Sask. 4.95

PACKAGED FORMS:

Divorce
☐B.C. 12.95 ☐Alberta 12.95 ☐Ontario   ☐Man.   ☐Sask.

Incorporation
☐B.C. 12.95 ☐Alberta 12.95 ☐Ontario 14.95

☐Man. 14.95 ☐Sask. 14.95 ☐Federal 9.95

☐Minute Books 16.50

Probate
☐B.C. Administration 14.95 ☐B.C. Probate 14.95 ☐Alberta 13.95 ☐Ontario 15.50

Sell Your Own Home
☐B.C. 4.95 ☐Alberta 4.95 ☐Ontario 4.95

☐Rental Form Kit (B.C., Alberta, Ontario, Sask.)   5.95

☐Have Your Made Your Will?   5.95

☐If You Love Me Put It In Writing   Contract Kit   9.95

☐If You Leave Me Put It In Writing   B.C. Separation Agreement Kit 14.95

NOTE: All prices subject to change without notice.

Books are available in book and department stores, or use the order form below.

Please enclose cheque or money order (plus sales tax where applicable) or give us your MasterCard or Visa Number (please include validation and expiry date).

(PLEASE PRINT)

Name _____

Address _____

City _____

Province _____ Postal Code _____

☐Visa/ ☐MasterCard Number _____

Validation Date _____ Expiry Date _____

If order is under $20.00, add $1.00 for postage and handling.

Please send orders to:

INTERNATIONAL SELF-COUNSEL PRESS LTD.   ☐Check here for free catalogue.
306 West 25th Street
North Vancouver, British Columbia
V7N 2G1

NATIONAL TITLES

____	Aids to Independence	$11.95
____	Assertiveness for Managers	8.95
____	Basic Accounting for the Small Business	5.95
____	Be a Better Manager	7.95
____	Business Guide to Effective Speaking	6.95
____	Business Guide to Telephone Systems	7.95
____	Business Writing Workbook	9.95
____	Buying (and Selling) a Small Business	6.95
____	Collection Techniques for the Small Business	4.95
____	Design Your Own Logo	9.95
____	Exporting from the U.S.A.	12.95
____	Family Ties that Bind	7.95
____	Financial Control for the Small Business	5.50
____	Financial Freedom on $5 a Day	7.95
____	Fundraising for Non-Profit Groups	5.50
____	Franchising in the U.S.	5.95
____	Getting Sales	14.95
____	How You Too Can Make a Million in the Mail Order Business	8.95
____	Immigrating to Canada	14.95
____	Immigrating to the U.S.A.	14.95
____	Keyboarding for Kids	7.95
____	Learn to Type Fast	
____	Managing Stress	7.95
____	Musician's Handbook	7.95
____	Parent's Guide to Day Care	5.95
____	Photography and the Law	7.95
____	Practical Guide to Financial Management	5.95
____	Ready-to-Use Business Forms	9.95
____	Resort Condos & Time Sharing	4.50
____	Retirement in the Pacific Northwest	4.95
____	Start and Run a Profitable Beauty Salon	14.95
____	Start and Run a Profitable Consulting Business	12.95
____	Start and Run a Profitable Craft Business	10.95
____	Start and Run a Profitable Home Typing Business	9.95
____	Start and Run a Profitable Restaurant	10.95
____	Start and Run a Profitable Retail Store	11.95
____	Start and Run a Profitable Video Store	10.95
____	Starting a Successful Business on West Coast	12.95
____	Upper Left-Hand Corner	10.95
____	Word Processing	8.95
____	Working Couples	5.50

STATE TITLES
Please indicate which state edition is required.

____ Divorce Guide
  ☐ Washington (with forms) 12.95 ☐ Oregon 11.95

_____ Employee/Employer Rights
☐ Washington 5.50

_____ Incorporation and Business Guide
☐ Washington 11.95 ☐ Oregon 11.95

_____ Landlord/Tenant Rights
☐ Washington 5.95   ☐ Oregon 6.95

_____ Marriage and Family Law
☐ Washington 4.50 ☐ Oregon 4.95

_____ Probate Guide
☐ Washington 9.95

_____ Real Estate Buying/Selling Guide
☐ Washington 5.95 ☐ Oregon 3.95

_____ Small Claims Court Guide
☐ Washington 4.50

_____ Wills
☐ Washington 5.50 ☐ Oregon 5.95

PACKAGED FORMS

_____ Divorce
☐ Oregon Set A (Petitioner) 12.95
☐ Oregon Set B (Co-Petitioners) 12.95

_____ If You Love Me — Put It In Writing 7.95

_____ Incorporation
☐ Washington 12.95 ☐ Oregon 12.95

_____ Probate
☐ Washington 9.95

_____ Will and Estate Planning Kit 5.95

_____ Rental Form Kit 3.95

All prices subject to change without notice.

☐ **Check here for free catalog**

(PLEASE PRINT)

NAME _____

ADDRESS _____

CITY _____

STATE _____

ZIP CODE _____

Check or Money Order enclosed. ☐
If order is under $20, add $1.50 for postage and handling.

Please send orders to:

SELF-COUNSEL PRESS INC.
1303 N. Northgate Way
Seattle, Washington, 98133
Phone: (206) 522-8383